First published in the UK in 2012, by Aurora Metro Press
67 Grove Avenue, Twickenham, Middlesex TW1 4HX
The Green Teen Cookbook © Aurora Metro Publications 2012
020 3261 0000 www.aurorametro.com

Introduction and compilation © Laurane Marchive 2012
In-house Editors: Cheryl Robson and Rebecca Gillieron
Cover design © Alice Marwick 2012
Photographs © Sarah Eisenfisz 2012
Illustrations © Dominic McInnes 2012

With special thanks to Edward Gosling, Sarah Eisenfisz, Dominic McInnes, all the people
from 18 Stonehouse who helped with the food tasting, and to all the contributors for the
donation of their recipes.

Thanks to Jack Timney, Martin Gilbert, Simon Smith, Lesley Mackay, Jackie Glasgow, Neil
Gregory, Richard Turk, Thomas Skinner, Sumedha Mane, Jeni Calnan, Neha Matkar.

Printed by Ashford Colour Press Ltd., Gosport, Hampshire.
ISBN: 978-1-906582-12-8

The Green Teen Cookbook

edited
by Laurane Marchive

Photographs
by Sarah Eisenfisz

Illustrations
by Dominic McInnes

AURORA METRO BOOKS

Contents

Part 2: Recipes That Don't Cost The Earth

Foreword

As a student, I always found it hard to cook cheap, healthy food on a day-to-day basis. My fridge was permanently empty and I could never be bothered to go to the shop in the evening to pick up ingredients to cook something fancy. I have to confess that for a long time, I only ate pasta with ready-made tomato paste. No oil, no butter. Maybe some salt. And it didn't taste good at all. So when I discovered (through different people, books and websites) that it was possible to cook good food without spending hours or loads of money on it, I was a bit surprised. I even realised that eating properly didn't cost much more than eating rubbish; often it cost a lot less.

But I was until very recently a teenager myself, and I know that many people, like me, don't really know how to cook healthily and on a budget. I didn't know what eating ethically meant either. So when I got the opportunity to put this cookbook together, I decided to find out.

Young people sent me recipes from all over the place, covering a wide range of different tastes and flavours. It was amazing how interested people were in the project. I asked teenagers to send me seasonal, ethical, healthy and affordable recipes. I also asked them to send articles about food and their own experiences. And it worked!

This book has been designed, written and produced by young people, for young people. And that's what makes it special: our recipes come from real teens who know what it's like to cook with little or no money. Some recipes are more or less expensive than others, some are fantastically healthy, some a little less so, but I think variety is important – and we all need a little treat, now and then, don't we?

I hope this cookbook helps you learn more about food, and I hope you enjoy the recipes! I tasted them all myself, and I have to say – I had a great time!

Laurane Marchive

Laurane studied journalism at the Institute of Political Sciences, Lille and French Modern Literature at the Sorbonne, Paris. After working as a journalist in France, Indonesia and India, she moved to London where she is now working as an editor, translator and rights agent. She also works as a freelance circus performer.

A Guide to Seasonal Cooking

A lot of our recipes are seasonal, and that's what makes them so great. It means you get the best food out of each season, but it also means you pay less for it. Small symbols on every recipe will tell you when to make them so they are fresh and will taste the best. As some of the recipes are good for more than one season, and some even slightly in between seasons, our symbols are mostly a rough guide to what's good when.

Spring, Spring, Spring! Little birds are in love, and maybe you're in love too! Or maybe not. But it doesn't matter, who needs love when we've got food? Rejoice in springy fruit and veg, winter is over, it's getting sunnier, so join the lambs frolicking in the fields!

Summer! "Follow the white rabbit", they say. But are you ready to take the trip? Summer will unfold for you wonders of taste and smell and yumminess, amazing fruit and mind-blowing veg. The time has come to worship the sunny season! So get ready to enjoy the ride...

Autumn! The Fall! Season of the romantics, of the falling leaves and endless melancholy. But have no fear, our recipes will cheer you up! Nothing fishy about our fish in a boot, it will lead you to the tastiest of all autumnal recipes. Just have faith in the old boot and follow it till the end of the season...

Winter! Although everything is cold and depressing, there are still some really good things to cook and keep you warm. (Since there is a shortage of fresh fruit and veg in winter, this is the one season when you might opt to use imported fruit and veg such as bananas.)

All year round! Eating seasonally is great, but of course some things are good all year round. So every time you see this little planet, you'll know that the food will be good whenever and wherever. Which also means that most of those recipes can be made out of cupboard ingredients... and that's quite convenient!

Measurement Conversion Table

American cup measurements

American	Imperial	Metric
1 cup flour	5 oz	142g
1 cup caster/granulated sugar	8 oz	227g
1 cup brown sugar	6 oz	170g
1 cup sultanas/raisins	7 oz	200g
1 cup ground almonds	4 oz	110g
1 cup uncooked rice	7 oz	200g
1 cup grated cheese	4 oz	113g
1 cup butter/margarine/lard	8 oz	227g
1 cup golden syrup	12 oz	341g

Weight

Imperial	Metric
½ oz	14 g
1 oz	28 g
2 oz	57 g
3 oz	85 g
4 oz	114 g
5 oz	142 g
10 oz	285 g
1 lb	455 g
2 lb	911 g
3 lb	1.36 kg

Oven Temperatures

Gas Mark	°F	°C
1	275°F	140°C
2	300°F	150°C
3	325°F	170°C
4	350°F	180°C
5	375°F	190°C
6	400°F	200°C
7	425°F	220°C
8	450°F	230°C
9	475°F	240°C

Liquid

Imperial	Metric	American
½ fl oz	15 ml	1 tbsp
1 fl oz	30 ml	1/8 cup
2 fl oz	60 ml	¼ cup
4 fl oz	120 ml	½ cup
8 fl oz	240 ml	1 cup
16 fl oz	480 ml	2 cups

Part 1
A Rough Guide To Ethical Eating

How to eat seasonally
by Andy Gold

As a young child I remember dreading the tomato. My first memories of this fruit are of a pale, poorly flavoured sad little rock, completely without life and ever-present on my dinner plate throughout the year. It was years later, one bright British summer, that I discovered something by the same name that was a delicious delight, ruby red and vibrant yellow, and bursting with juices.

Although both were tomatoes in name, the former was the sad supermarket staple, grown year round and picked whilst still green, only turning red later on. Shipped – or worse still – flown to our supermarket shelves, it has become ever present at the disappointing seasonless dinner table. The tasty version was a local British variety, picked at the height of summer, in full ripeness and had travelled a short distance to my plate. Someone once said to me the best way to learn to dance is just to start dancing ... and the same advice works for starting to eat more seasonal food. You'll notice the sheer delight the moment you eat something that is bang in season and you'll find that you won't want to stop.

I did an interview for TV a couple of years ago with Alan Titchmarsh where I explained that all seasonal food reminds me of the energising intensity of a summer holiday. Seasonal tomatoes are delicious for breakfast on toast; at lunch time in a salad in the sun with a drizzle of balsamic vinegar; at home in a warm dish with chorizo, shallots, garlic and some sherry vinegar or in the evening underneath a whole fresh sardine stuffed full of herbs and lemon. No nights in front of the television, no "I can't be bothered" – just savouring every moment until – gone for another year.

> ... the moment you eat something that is bang in season you'll find that you won't want to stop.

Summer is also the time I gorge myself every year on asparagus (last year a bunch of us did a 'pick your own' and then cooked the spears quickly in boiling water and then dipped them in soft boiled eggs – try it, probably the world's most amazing soldiers). Jersey Royal potatoes and artichokes, soon followed later in the same season by aubergines and courgettes, all on the barbecue with big slices of halloumi cheese. Radishes just washed and sprinkled with sea salt can be wolfed down like bright pink mini savoury apples. Crunchy cucumber and watercress sandwiches with bread that's been covered in cream cheese with herbs, garlic and chilli in it. And then there's berries, all kinds of wonderful berries, fresh from the bushes, the easiest foraging in the world and perfect for a picnic. As if summer isn't fantastic enough anyway ...

There's a reason why all of this fruit and veg tastes better for being seasonal and local. Tests show that a leaf like spinach loses around half of its nutrients in the first twenty-four hours after it's harvested. Along with those nutrients also disappears a lot of the flavour. Across all fruit and veg it's the same story. The longer it takes to get from field to fork the less flavourful your mouthful will be. And it's that *wow* factor that makes going back to far-flung fruits and very tired veg a bit of a disappointment, and not only will your taste buds be missing the flavour, your body won't be getting the same nutritious hit of goodness either.

> **The longer it takes to get from field to fork the less flavourful your mouthful will be.**

Once you've spent a year enjoying eating seasonally you'll find yourself starting to look forward to different foods as the seasons change. It's easy enough to look forward to spring and summer but let's face it anything that makes us excited about autumn and winter has got to be a good thing. I might curse the first day in October or November that I find myself cycling home in the dark through the rain (or occasionally even snow!) but at least I'm cheered by knowing that when I pass by the market near my house to shop for my tea, I'll be able to pick up sweet satisfying parsnips and beetroots or some aniseedy fennel for some roasted restoration when I get in the door. It's as if nature knows what I need and has prepared stuff that is best done in the oven, warming up my whole house in the process.

It's wild mushroom and truffle time too in autumn and although I might not be a millionaire (yet!) a summer truffle grated on a poached egg is a part of the millionaire's lifestyle I can afford, if I do the work myself.

Some of the best meats also start to come into season too as autumn turns into winter – first lovely plump well-fed rabbits and then as the leaves fall off the trees, pigeon, partridge and pheasant! And summer isn't the end of the great 'event' food either, the sexy sunny days of summer, picnics and barbecues, give way to warm fires and dark candlelit nights of fondues and feasts. When it comes to food, the celebration of Christmas in Britain, is as good as anywhere in the world. However, there is no reason why, in a country with a climate as wonderfully varied through the seasons as ours, we can't have a meal that is just as much of an event at any point in the year.

I ate my first mussels at the age of twelve – I scoffed a bowl twice the size of my head. A new tradition, and an event to look forward to in my house, is building a fire as soon as winter gives way to spring and having a load of mates round for big bowls of these delicious creatures cooked in a big iron pan. I've got a bit of a taste for oysters and fried squid too and pints of prawns from the Atlantic. All are treats best enjoyed in the cold months and a reason to be cheerful, to get together with friends and savour the cold months.

Seasonal food isn't just better for you, tastier and more fun, it's also cheaper. I took a group of young people I was teaching to cook down to one of my favourite places to buy seasonal veg, the always animated Ridley Road Market, in Hackney, East London. We had in hand a receipt for a big purchase of fruit and vegetables from a local supermarket and proceded to buy a big sack of fruit from Pitch 2's Fruit and Veg Man, Tony, at a staggeringly low price.

"How's it so cheap?" one of my students asked (with her jaw on the floor in surprise at just how cheap, I should add). "Yesterday that sweetcorn was in the ground in Essex just outside London," explained Tony.

"There's no trick to growing it, just needs some land and some patience. In the afternoon a van came by and a load of corn was picked and put on the back of it and driven into town. I picked it up first thing this morning and now it's here with you in time for you to take some home for lunch. It's cheap 'cos it's simple and no one's had to do too much work to get it here."

> ... **more local seasonal food means less energy spent transporting produce around.**

Unfortunately, with their central distribution centres and need for intense organisation that's a simplicity and a speed supermarkets just can't match. If you want to take Tony's Pitch 2 Challenge he's easy to find (it's the nearest fruit and veg stall to the Kingsland Road as you enter the market). If you're not in the Hackney area there are local markets near you with traders just like Tony. As an added bonus, if you become a regular face at someone's stall you'll probably start getting the benefit of discounts and other juicy bonuses. Support your local traders and they'll remember you better than a corporate loyalty card ever can.

In the big picture, we all understand how reducing our carbon footprint is good for the planet and really important if we don't want to see the earth's climate changing at any more an alarming rate than it already is. You don't need to be a rocket scientist to work out that more local seasonal food means less energy spent transporting produce around.

Whenever you're reading this, I can guarantee that whatever the season, there'll be something amazing in the shops. To find out what's getting us excited today, check out our website and while you're online you can add to the fantastic recipes in this book by googling up some extra ideas yourself.

Andy is a chef and cookery teacher. He works for Shoreditch Trust, managing the Blue Marble Training programme which helps people with aspiration, passion for food, and untapped potential to access careers in the food industry. To learn more about Blue Marble Training visit: www.shoreditchtrust.org.uk / Blue-Marble-Trust

Why eat healthily?
by Sarah Veniard

Achieving balance within our mind, body and spirit is a challenge that can sometimes seem overwhelming. With so many choices about which form of exercise we should be practising, and which foods we should and should not be eating, we can find ourselves going into system overload. The important thing to remember is that we are all unique. Each and every one of us is tuned differently, with varying needs and desires, different metabolisms, and we all need to find our own path to achieving an all round sense of well-being.

Following a healthy, balanced diet may seem like a challenge if you don't know where to begin. All through your life your body goes through changes, especially when you are evolving from adolescence into adulthood so it's important to take good care of yourself, and the first step towards achieving this is to have a healthy diet.

> ... it's important to take good care of yourself, and the first step towards achieving this is to have a healthy diet.

Whatever diet you have chosen to follow, whether you eat meat, or have chosen a vegetarian, vegan, or any other special diet, it is essential that you are getting all of your nutrients in the most balanced way possible. Not doing this will have negative effects on your immune system and energy levels. If you get it right, you can be at the peak of health. Once you know how, it's easy to cover all of the important food groups, and to do so on a budget.

It is vital that you have enough iron coming from your food. I recommend eating an abundance of delightful deep green leafy veg, such as spinach, and my absolute favourite, kale. Kale is loaded with calcium, essential for healthy bones and teeth, an element that rarely appears in fruit and vegetables, as well as vitamin C, iron, manganese, potassium and beta-carotene, which is an important nutrient for good vision. This superveg also contains high levels of chlorophyll, a plant pigment present in all green leafy veg. Researchers claim that the molecular structure of chlorophyll is similar to haemoglobin, which is used for carrying blood around the body. Not only does it increase oxygen availability in the body, it helps with the rapid assimilation of amino acids and boosts your immune system. With that knowledge, feel inspired to eat as many of these lean green delicacies as you can and you will be a high-powered healthy super being!

A fine balance of B vitamins, vitamin C, vitamin E, amino acids and calcium is important. Eat a good variety of fruit and vegetables – it's easy to get your five a day once you begin the cycle. And you will feel more balanced and beautiful than ever!

Introducing some superfoods into your diet is a positive step and can be fun too. You'll experience increased energy, immunity and feelings of well-being. Indigenous people have been eating superfoods for thousands of years with a firm understanding of their healing powers. So this is an opportunity for you to tap into that ancient knowledge and reap the benefits.

> Indigenous people have been eating superfoods for thousands of years with a firm understanding of their healing powers.

Maca, originating from the Andes, has a number of benefits. For a start, it is a great oxygenator of the blood, which helps athletes to perform better, (imagine the effect this can have on your studies!), it heightens your immunity, enhances your stamina levels, and is a hormonal balancer, great for alleviating menstrual pains. Also, it is an adaptogen, which means it lets the body adapt to many negative ailments. Maca is also a great natural source of calcium.

Raw Cacao, is the purest and healthiest way to eat chocolate. It is a natural antidepressant due to the seratonin precursor tryptophan. It is also the second highest antioxidant food in the world and it is an appetite suppressant, so it can be useful in helping you to lose weight in a healthy way. Furthermore, it has the highest magnesium content of any food.

Spirulina is considered the ultimate superfood. It is a complete protein, containing eight essential amino acids, the highest protein food in the world (very useful for vegetarians in particular). Also high in antioxidants, it contains almost everything we need in the way of vitamins and minerals, in perfect ratios for the human body. Spirulina is also rich in essential fatty acids. For more info on superfoods, check out websites such as Naturally Green, and Funky Raw. (**www.naturallygreen.co.uk** / **www.funkyraw.com**)

Another way to boost energy levels is to incorporate more raw foods into our diets. With a fully or predominantly raw food diet, you'll experience greater emotional stability, mental clarity and enhanced immunity. It is a fun and healthy way of losing weight, and you can find yourself looking and feeling years younger, with clear skin and twinkling eyes. With all of that new found energy... *wow...* others will naturally gravitate towards your new sparkling aura!

So why shouldn't we cook our food? Natural foods in their pure, uncooked state still have all of their enzymes, proteins, fats, vitamins and minerals intact. As soon as you heat food above 105°F (though new research is pointing toward a figure more in the region of 150°F), the molecular structure of the nutrients are altered, and the body can no longer recognise them as something that can be utilised. This change in molecular structure leads to the creation of numerous unnatural and potentially dangerous chemical compounds, including carcinogens.

It has been claimed that the process of cooking our food can destroy between 30% and 97% of the vitamins, depending on the cooking method and temperature. It is interesting to remember that we are the only species that cooks our food and simultaneously, the only species that is plagued with an array of chronic diseases, including obesity, cancer, arthritis, and diabetes. However, you don't need to eat only raw food to get the benefits, try eating around 50% of your food raw and see how it works for you.

The next step to becoming healthier, is to have a go at growing your own food. You do not need a lot of space. If you have a little garden, sow some salad seeds, plant some herbs, it's so simple. Or maybe add a window box for an attractive edible growing space. If you include some nectar-rich flowers to attract beneficial insects, they'll act as natural predators, feeding on the insects that will attempt to eat your crops before you do!

It has been claimed that the process of cooking our food can destroy between 30% and 97% of the vitamins...

It's a good idea to build a connection with the plant world and develop a more natural way of being. Plants have a lot of benefits – why not try sprouting? Experts say that the benefits of sprouted pulses, nuts and grains are supremely understated. Pound for pound, they are more nutritious than any other food. They can also be eaten fresher than any other food as they grow vigorously right up until the moment you eat them! Amazingly, sprouts have a complete nutritional profile, and some say that this means we could live on these and nothing else! You can eat them raw so they're perfect for anyone on a living foods diet.

The process of sprouting actually increases the quality, quantity and variety of nutrients available to us, and it's so easy. So get yourselves a sprouting jar. It's a super cheap way to create an abundance of tasty beansprouts to eat as salads, or sprinkle over your dishes. They are ready to eat in about three days, and make you feel amazing!

Enjoy your journey towards better health – you'll soon be cruising through those essays with increased brainpower. With a better relationship with your body too, you'll be on the way to becoming a healthier and happier individual. So why not invite some friends over, get yourselves in the kitchen and experiment? Your friends will soon see how exciting, varied and delicious a healthy diet can be...

Sarah is a self-employed garden designer, who uses the principles of Permaculture in her designs, creating sustainable and environmentally friendly gardens that may produce food and will attract an abundance of beneficial wildlife. You can visit her website at: http://sarahssecretgarden.wordpress.com

What is fair trade?

by Barry Hallinger

The Fair trade movement was an initiative starting in the 1960s that aimed to create a system to combat the inherent inequalities rife in the world trading system. These inequalities discriminated against producer countries, which usually had much lower national wealth, by paying unrealistically low prices for products to increase consumer interest in 'developed' countries. In the 1970s and 80s competitive trading resulted in price deflation whereby companies could lower the prices of their products in order to compete in a supply and demand market: "The total loss for developing countries due to falling commodity prices has been estimated by the Food and Agricultural Organisation to total almost $250 billion during the 1980 - 2002 period". (FINE 2006) The people most seriously affected were agricultural farmers who had to procure more land to grow and increase output – usually for no financial gain.

Fairtrade certification is for products that sell at above market price with the aim that the extra money is to go directly to the farmers and their communities. These better prices improve working conditions, reduce child labour and increase the sustainability of trade in the long term. Fairtrade products also support development projects, such as the building of schools and hospitals and reduce environmental impact from poor farming practices. If you buy Fairtrade products you are standing up for basic human rights and sending the message that it is not acceptable to ignore the rights of producers who suffer from the conventional trading system.

The Fairtrade scheme is an attempt to address these market failures by providing farmers and producers with a reasonable price for their crop, as well as business advice, access to the 'developing' nation markets and better trading conditions: "in these respects at least, the role of Fairtrade is effective..." (Ronchi 2006)

You might think that you cannot afford the extra pennies for that bag of coffee but in reality, current market prices do not properly reflect the true costs associated with production and only a well-managed stable minimum price system can cover environmental and social production costs and that is the aim of the Fairtrade certification scheme.

However... while the fair trade movement is a monumental step in the right direction against the consolidation of wealth for a few, and is actively campaigning for basic human rights and sustainable development, it is not without its critics.

It is argued that by paying more for products, this creates a false subsidy which harms farmers in the long term and that it prevents what is really needed – a fundamental change in the trading system. This, in my opinion, is something that must be addressed if the movement itself wants to be fully legitimate and sustainable. The main drawback in claiming Fairtrade's full effectiveness would be a lack of evidence demonstrating that participating in the scheme produces a net positive economic result for Fairtrade product suppliers, and it may, in fact, have a negative effect on non-Fairtrade farmers.

There are few reliable studies attempting to measure impacts on Fairtrade farmers and a control of matched non-Fairtrade farmers, from the time Fairtrade was introduced. And there appear to be none assessing which of the many aid organisations involved is responsible for any changes observed. This failure of Fairtrade monitoring organisations, FLO international and FLO-cert to check the social, economic and environmental benefits of producer countries, raises questions of why the companies are still not transparent and challenges the legitimacy of the various umbrella companies that regulate it.

> If you buy Fairtrade products you are standing up for basic human rights and sending the message that it is not acceptable to ignore the rights of producers who suffer from the conventional trading system.

Although these are big issues that must be addressed in the coming years, philosophically and practically, Fairtrade is a beneficial trading system for the future sustainability of the human race. Consumption should be based on production not false market competition, and workers, no matter where, should benefit from their hard work, see their community grow and not be exploited so you can save a few pennies on a bunch of bananas.

If you agree with the principle and practice of Fairtrade certification you can check which products are available locally to you on this website:
http://www.fairtrade.net

FINE (2006). Business Unusual. Brussels: Fair Trade Advocacy Office
Ronchi, L. (2006). "Fairtrade and Market Failures in Agricultural Commodity Markets". World Bank Policy Research Working Paper 4011, September 2006.

Barry graduated in 2009 with a BA Hons in Social Anthropology and since then has helped build a school and teach English in the Nepalese Himalayas. Since coming to London he has started a community-based project called 'Ethnogenic' which supports friend-based markets and raises money for charity projects. He is inspired to try and create a more realistic and fair economy by removing the artificial distance between producer and supplier of commodities. He plans to study a Masters in International Relations and Enviromental Law.

How to source local products and avoid air miles

or why eating a 'Knobby Russet' can make you feel good about yourself and save the world at the same time...

by Edward Gosling

Californian oranges? Tuna from off the coast of Chile? Lamb from New Zealand? Avocados from Spain? Mangos from Pakistan? Coffee from Kenya? The world on your doorstep. Push your trolley down the aisles and take your pick. Right? It's all so shiny looking: different colours, exotic food – you can buy strawberries in winter, apples all year round. Supermarkets certainly seem to be offering us more diverse options from... well... just about everywhere! But can we rest easy in our eating, or does this apparent greater choice come at a cost?

There's an obvious reason why eating locally produced food is better – it has a far lower environmental impact. All those foods from all over the world mean a lot of unnecessary fossil fuels burned every day just to get them in front of you and into your saucepan or onto your plate. Try the 100-mile diet and rest assured that the food you're eating isn't adding to your carbon footprint. Eating local produce keeps you connected to the seasons as you are only eating what's around that month – this might even push you to experiment a bit and try some new things instead of just resorting to that tried and tested dish you make on autopilot. It's also going to be a lot fresher. Local fruit and vegetables can stay in the ground or on the tree those few extra days, which is when they really soak up loads of flavour and nutrients. It's not only healthier for you but poses less risk – food transported long distance has a much higher chance of becoming contaminated.

At a time when globalisation is trying to suck us up into its oh-so-tempting giant homogenous unquestioning approach to the world – obey obey obey, buy more, obey, give up your individuality, buy the same things, look the same, be the same, obey obey obey – eating locally does something positive for the community around you. Buying straight from farmers on your doorstep supports the local economy, which may mean you get that money back easier, so you're really helping to support yourself. It preserves green spaces from development and it cuts out the middleman.

Why give faceless supermarkets all the cash? Why not instead meet someone who cares about the food they're growing because it's their livelihood? Giving local farmers money directly restores the balance of consumer to supplier and means that you have a personal human interaction with someone, instead of a robot voice telling you that there is an unexpected item is in the bagging area. And you don't just support farmers in the UK, you also support farmers in developing countries. If someone in the UK offers to buy an African or South American farmer's produce at a higher price than local people will give him, the farmer is obviously going to sell for more. Hey, he's got a wife to support, kids to educate, a couple of debts to pay off ... But this can mean that people in developing countries have to pay inflated prices for food that is produced locally to them, which really isn't very fair.

> Giving local farmers money directly restores the balance of consumer to supplier and means that you have a personal human interaction with someone.

And if you're feeling bad for the farmer (thinking something like: it's a capitalist free market economy, why should we expect him to get less than he could for his crop? What right do we have to interfere?) then you should know that many farms in developing countries are now owned by large organisations or banks. Attracted by the financial opportunities that can be made by buying up vast tracts of cheap land, exploiting expendable, unregulated labour forces and selling off produce to richer countries, they reap huge profits. The economies of scale they're able to implement mean small farmers can't compete and are forced to sell off their land, perpetuating an oppressive system further. The farmers then work on these massive estates for a pitiful wage. So the rich get richer, food prices go up, more people starve and you get food that isn't as fresh and tasty as you could get if you just went two miles down the road. They call this a lose, lose, lose situation. Don't be a part of it.

It may seem like when you go to the supermarket you're getting more choice, but appearances can be deceiving. How many types of apples can you name? *Granny Smith, Pink Lady, Cox*...? Did you know that there are over 7,500 different types of apple in the world? In the 19th century in Britain alone there were over 2,000 different varieties to choose from including the *Hoary Morning, Blenheim Orange, Knobby Russet* and *Laxton's Epicure*. 'You could have eaten a different one every day for more than six years.' (BBC: 16.06.11) Today, we import over 70% of the apples we eat into the UK. What happened? Well, small shops turned into large chains and they stopped buying local produce. All those delicious individual apples weren't valued and instead mass-produced giant orchards with mile after mile of the same variety took over to cater to big retailers. How boring!

Recent studies have shown that eating locally is better for air quality and lowering pollution than eating organically. And – a big thing to think about – it is also much cheaper. When you eat locally produced food you don't have to pay for transportation, fuel, the truck driver's wage, or for all the people handling and packaging the food. Food prices are rising above inflation around the world, so for me, spending less on my weekly shop is a hell of an incentive, especially when you're helping out the environment, local farmers and people around the world – and getting something fresher, tastier and healthier all at the same time.

Ed is an editor and circus performer, which means he likes to read and also to play with fire. He lives in London and has a habit of accidentally cooking food for fifteen people. He's currently cooking quite a lot of red cabbage and believes the world would be a better place if the socialist revolution swept away the decaying vanguard of elite right-wing remnants of feudalism ...

Organic food
by Chloe Harris

To go organic or not? Is it healthier and more nutritious? Or simply tastier? Is the whole thing a scam to get you to pay more for nothing? How do you decide?

The first thing we need to understand is just how organic food is different. Food can only be certified as organic if it follows certain rules of production. It must be grown in soil that is restricted in the use of pesticides. Organic farmers develop soil that is rich in nutrients naturally and encourage insects and other wildlife to help reduce pests. Artificial chemical fertilisers are not allowed. Farmers must try to develop healthy soil by natural means such as rotating crops. This results in soil being more nutritious and able to support micro-organisms and so organic farming is definitely kinder to the environment.

Many people now agree that on a factory farm where animals are treated as if they were commodities with no quality of life, the food which is produced is not going to be of the best quality. In contrast, organic farmers treat animals humanely and do not use drugs such as antibiotics or worming agents. Instead, farmers must find natural ways of keeping the animals healthy. Genetic modifying is also prohibited on organic farms. According to many pro-organic farmers and consumers, all these factors result in organic food being more nutritious and having a wonderful, fresh and tasty flavour, compared with the bland taste of non-organic products. Organic farming scores well here too with its respect for living creatures.

Organic food is not processed using colorants, additives, preservatives or irradiation. As some people are sensitive to or have adverse reactions to these processes and additives, organic food is a safer bet to avoid these kinds of health problems.

So what's not to like? The biggest disadvantage is the *cost* of organic food. As it is more expensive to produce, it's costlier to buy and this means people often associate it with wealthier lifestyles. Organic food also lasts a shorter time than non-organic food as it contains no preservatives. This means its shelf life is reduced and it goes to waste if it's not used quickly. This adds to the cost for farmers and shops which sell organic products and puts the price up for consumers. In addition to the cost, both scientists and the Department of Health deny there are *any* health or nutritional benefits: "Current evidence shows that organic food is not significantly different in terms of nutrition from food produced conventionally". (FSA Study/ London School of Hygiene & Tropical Medicine, 2009) So it's hard for the individual to know what to believe.

A more cost-effective way of going organic is to grow your own food. My family have tried this in our own garden. We've grown beans and asparagus. And they were delicious! In my own experience, homegrown organic food tastes better and obviously costs less than buying it from the shops. Growing your own food is also a great way of minimising waste. It means you're more likely to eat food quickly so that it does not go bad. If you have a garden, you could give it a go. Or rent a public allotment near you and start planting! There are many self-help books and websites on organic gardening to assist you.

In my quest to find out more about organic food, I asked some people on the streets of my home town what they think of the issue:

17 year-old Nitin Patel said: "In my household we like to buy organic occasionally since it tastes better and is better for the environment. When I get my own place I will carry on buying organic. I find that if you choose your products wisely, if you stop over-eating and buying ready-made products that cost loads of money, buying organic food isn't much more expensive than eating unhealthy cheap food in the end. But you need to learn how to eat properly again, and for some of us, it's not an easy one..."

> Some say that organic food isn't really better for you. Maybe it isn't. So what? Treating the animals and nature iself more humanely is a good enough reason to buy organic food, isn't it?

33 year-old Wayne Brown said: "I like the taste of organic food and I like to splash out once in a while but could not afford to eat organic everyday! On top of that, I'm not even sure it's better for your health. And they say that you can never really know what is organic and what isn't. Because if you've got an organic crop in one field and a non-organic one in the next one, the wind can blow the non-organic seeds towards the organic field. I hear that a lot. I don't know if it's true but it makes sense. And it makes me doubt the very concept of organic food..."

60 year-old Pamela Ross said: "I have heard that organic food is better for the environment and I think it's a good idea to treat animals well rather than making them suffer just so that we can afford to eat them! I think organic farming is a good thing and I eat organic meat and milk at the least. Some say that organic food isn't really better for you. Maybe it isn't. So what? Treating the animals and nature iself more humanely is a good enough reason to buy organic food, isn't it? The way we grow food nowadays and the way we treat animals is shameful. If organic farming can change that, whether better for health or not, I don't care. It's a good thing anyway."

19 year-old Sally Smith told me, "It's just too expensive! I'm strapped for cash most of the time and would rather spend my disposable income on going out and having a laugh with my mates!"

So where are you on the organic spectrum? Total non-organic consumer? A little occasionally? Or full-blown organic all the time? Most people seem to be hovering around the middle. At the end of the day, it's up to you, but I hope I have helped you weigh up the pros and cons to make up your own mind!

Chloe lives in Wales and is currently attending high school. She is really into cooking, especially her favourite food – pear sorbet. She has three dogs and two cats.

The ethics of vegetarianism

by Sherry West

Vegetarianism, of course, is as old as the hills. Most people in India are vegetarians since both Hindus and Jains espouse a vegetarian diet and a philosophy of non-violence towards animals. For millennia, a large proportion, if not a majority, of the human race, has chosen to forego meat and fish in favour of vegetables.

Our ancestors were hunter-gatherers who ate mostly fruit and berries, roots and grubs, with occasional supplements of mammoth, kangaroo, and alligator. Like chimpanzees, we have evolved to feed omnivorously. Our teeth and guts testify to our readiness.

However, once people took up farming and there was a surplus of food, mere survival was supplanted by lifestyle choices. People had time to think about the good, the bad, and the spiritual – the quest for the meaning of life began. Today, vegetarianism is mainly a lifestyle choice although people choose it for a variety of reasons – religious, political, economic, cultural as well as health.

> …it's not hard to stay healthy without meat. A reasonable variety of fruit, pulses, nuts and milk will provide everything the body needs.

Certainly, it's not hard to stay healthy without meat. A reasonable variety of fruit, pulses, nuts and milk will provide everything the body needs. Protein, fat, carbohydrates, vitamins, amino acids, etc, can all be hoovered up by the careful Veggie.

Vegetarians tend to have lower cholesterol, lower blood pressure and fewer diseases than meat-eaters. Studies show that a vegetarian diet is less likely to result in heart disease, diabetes, colon cancer and obesity than eating meat. There is also less risk of food contamination (although the outbreak of e-coli in Northern Germany shows that plants such as lettuce and beansprouts can be sources too). Eggs are common sources of salmonella.

Some vegetarians choose to eat dairy products, others will forego meat but eat fish and seafood. Vegans refuse any food that contains animal products, which includes cheese (contains rennet from a sheep's stomach) and white sugar (contains bone char as a whitener). They may also refuse to wear clothing which is made from animals or which includes products, chemicals and dyes tested on animals.

Many argue that vegetarianism is more environmentally friendly too. The vast increase in cattle herds for the beef market has led to a huge amount of land being given over to cattle rather than growing plants and trees and the incredible amount of methane which the cows emit adds to the build up of greenhouse gases in the atmosphere each year. Equally, the demand for fish has emptied the oceans and affected marine eco-systems in many parts of the world, bringing many species to the point of extinction.

So why not try going veggy? Firstly, be aware that when you stop eating meat and/or fish, your body will naturally crave it. This is where it is important to be strong and persist. A vital part of this process is ensuring that you are replacing all the vitamins, minerals and nutrients that you once got from meat and fish with vegetarian alternatives.

Meat provides a lot of protein, though not in the correct form for our bodies to be able to digest it all successfully. It is also very difficult to break down, therefore the digestion process is extremely slow, which can lead to feelings of low energy and heaviness. It is advisable to replace this protein source with other veggie alternatives, such as soya products like tofu (beancurd a little like feta cheese) or tempeh (a kind of veggy burger).

Other great sources of protein include beans, pulses and nuts. Why not make sumptuous falafels, and serve them with warm pitta bread, salad and natural yoghurt? Or transport your new experimental cuisine to the Far East and make a lentil dahl with cashews, served with rice and greens. There are many good alternatives to pasta and pizza, including noodles, couscous, mushrooms and wild rice. For more ideas, see the recipes in this book or check out websites like: www.vegsoc.org.uk and www.cookveg.co.uk

Flexitarian

For those of you who can't give up meat altogether, try cutting down to a couple of times a week and alternate between meat, fish and veggie dishes. Above all, do not eat meat more than two or three times a week and ensure that it is of good quality. A good plan is to eat less meat and fish but spend a little more on organic options which are not processed and pumped full of chemicals and additives. Cheap meat is commonly pumped full of water to increase its weight. This produces poor quality meat and is in no way beneficial for your health. With less meat in your diet, you'll probably feel more energised.

When it comes to fish, be careful which fish you choose as cod, haddock, blue fin tuna, sole and even shark are on the endangered list. Fishing quotas have resulted in nearly a quarter of all fish being discarded because they are the wrong species and deep-sea trawlers are removing bottom-dwelling fish which don't even start breeding until they are twenty to thirty years old, decimating stocks. To find out more, check out the red list on the Greenpeace website: (www.greenpeace.org/international/seafood).

Finally, I hope I've helped you realise that your choice of food is not simply a personal matter but a political and moral choice too, as it affects the environment, farmers and fishermen in other parts of the world and most of all, the lives and futures of other living creatures.

Processed foods and additives
and the myths about E numbers
by Sophia Robson

With all the stories in the newspapers linking food additives and E numbers to obesity, cancer and hyperactive behaviour, they must be harmful, right? And if we want to live a long, healthy life, we should listen to all those health gurus advising us to cut them out completely, shouldn't we?

The answer is both yes, and no. Even if we want to avoid them, it's not that easy to cut food additives out of our diets completely, as food manufacturers are using them in all sorts of ways, either to extend the shelf life of a food product or just to make something appeal to our senses, so we buy more of it. There are more than 300 different additives currently in use and they occur in over 50% of all supermarket products.

So, as most of us buy our food from supermarkets, we need to understand more about the mountains of E numbers we're busy consuming. And I've come to realise from researching this article that there are a lot of myths circulating around food additives and E numbers. Some of these additives are actually good for us, for example E300 is essentially Vitamin C.

> ... even if you ate an entirely organic diet you would still consume E numbers

Furthermore, even if you ate an entirely organic diet you would still consume E numbers as many come from natural sources. And most shockingly to me, I even learnt that twenty of these additives are produced by the human body itself, which means they can't all be bad.

So what is an additive anyway and why are they used?

Additives are generally used to keep food looking good during storage and transportation, right up until the time it goes into your shopping basket. They are numbered according to category and these are some of the main groups:

- Colourings (E100- E199)
- Preservatives (E200- E299)
- Antioxidants (E300- E399)
- Thickeners, stabilisers and emulsifiers (E400- E499)
- Acidity regulators and anti-caking agents (E500-E599)-
- Flavour enhancers (E600- E699)
- Surface coating agents and sweeteners (E900- E999)

> ... twenty of these additives are produced by the human body itself, which means they can't all be bad.

Colourings: To avoid the loss of natural colour that occurs during food processing, colourings are often added. These not only help make the pre-cooked or processed food look more appealing but apparently make it 'taste' better, as we tend to 'taste' with our eyes. They keep the product looking bright and fresh, rather than grey and unattractive, persuading us it's good to eat. Some people think the addition of artificial colourings is unnecessary. Others claim they cause adverse reactions, especially Tartrazine (E102) a yellow dye that is in many products and can cause asthma attacks and Red 2G (E128) which is used to colour meat and burgers and has been linked to cancer.

> **Colourings ... not only help make the food look more appealing but apparently make it 'taste' better ...**

Preservatives: To avoid microbial growth (mould) during the many days that food is stored or transported, preservatives need to be added. Preservatives are often used in cheeses, margarines, low-fat spreads, dressings, fruit and bakery products. Without the use of preservatives, the incidence of food poisoning would be much higher. They reduce the risk of getting sick from bacteria like salmonella, for example.

Antioxidants: Antioxidants are added to foods to stop them reacting to the oxygen in the air and going off. While they prevent foods from going rancid and extend their shelf-life, it's been discovered that they may also prevent diseases such as arthritis and cancer, offering potential health benefits.

Thickeners, stabilisers, and emulsifiers: Thickeners make food bulkier. They are used to increase the thickness of a liquid product without changing its other properties. Stabilisers keep the products stable during storage and transportation, preventing the ingredients from separating. Emulsifiers help ingredients to mix together, e.g. in mayonnaise the emulsifier keeps the oil and water from separating. Gelling agents help make foods stick together in the form of a jelly. Pectin is the most common gelling agent (E440), it's used by many people to make fruit into jam.

Acidity regulators and anti-caking agents: Acidity regulators, or pH control agents, are added to change or maintain a product's pH state (acidity or basicity). They are used in fizzy drinks, fruit and bakery products as well as some canned goods to prevent botulism. Common pH control agents are acetic acid and citric acid. The typical Western diet is already considered to be too high in acid producing food like meat, eggs and dairy and too low in alkaline producing food such as fresh vegetables. The human body needs a balance of both acid and alkaline food to remain healthy. It's claimed that the addition of so much acid to our diet can lead to a breakdown in our immune system and other health problems. An anti-caking agent is added to powders or granulated products to make them flow better. They are usually added to powdered soups and drinks in vending machines to prevent the formation of lumps.

Flavour Enhancers: Flavourings are added to mimic a particular flavour in a particular food. The average flavouring can contain dozens of ingredients. Flavour enhancers are added to a wide variety of foods such as crisps, pre-cooked dinners and sauces to make them taste better. For example, MSG or Monosodium Glutamate (E621) is often added to foods such as sausages and soups. There are health concerns about its long-term effects and links with obesity.

Surface coating agents and sweeteners: To make a food look shiny or give it a protective coating, a surface coating agent is applied. A sweetener is a substance which is used to create a sweet taste to a food or drink. People are keen to avoid sugar, so alternative sweeteners such as Aspartame (E951) and Saccharin (E954) are now used as they are low in calories and better for teeth. There is ongoing controversy about how safe these intense sweeteners really are. Sorbitol (E420) is a compound made chemically from glucose and used as a bulk sweetener to replace sugar in many products.

So as you can see there are an extensive number of additives, and they're mostly used to change foods from their natural states for our convenience or safety. Technically, milk is a processed food as it's pasteurized to kill the bacteria and then homogenized to keep the fats from separating. By chemically altering food products, the manufacturers give us a much wider range of foods to choose from, which simply wouldn't have been possible in the past.

Another fact to be aware of is that the many processes involved in bringing pre-cooked and processed food to the table such as canning, freezing, dehydrating and irradiating our food can lead to a loss of nutrients. So if you have the kind of lifestyle that sees you eating processed foods on a regular basis, and you want to reduce the amount of additives you're eating, there are definitely some processed foods you should avoid:

• breads and pastas made from refined white flour instead of whole grains
• packaged high-calorie snack foods such as crisps and sweets
• frozen fish fingers and frozen dinners that are high in salt
• packaged cakes and cookies
• boxed meal mixes that are high in fat and salt
• sugary breakfast cereals
• processed meats
• canned foods with large amounts of fat or salt

Next time you shop for those convenient ready meals or TV dinners, opt for products that are made with whole grains, low in calories, and low in saturated fat and salt. Avoid anything made with hydrogenated vegetable oils as this can raise cholesterol. And if you're really worried about the overload of food additives in your diet, why not buy fresh food from your local market, or maybe even start your own vegetable patch?

Sophia is at Sydney University studying a BA in Arts. She loves cooking and eating out and is an avid fan of Master Chef.

Freeganism
by Rhea Kantam

I have always been told by my parents and teachers not to waste food, that waste is bad for the environment, and to think of all the people in the world who go hungry every day because they are not as lucky as I am. So I was really shocked when I learned that supermarkets throw away millions of tonnes of food every year.

When I first heard about freeganism I wasn't sure what to think. Initially, I thought it was just about eating from bins and that seemed wrong but when I learned more about it, I discovered that it was an environmental movement that encourages living off society's waste, which really made sense to me. So when I heard people from my college were going to try it, I thought I would go along to see what it was like. We decided to go to a supermarket nearby because we'd heard that the supermarkets were the worst offenders for waste and we thought we'd find the biggest range of food there. We set off just after nightfall. Before we arrived, I was half expecting lots of rotting food in huge bins but it wasn't like that at all. The food was neatly packaged and most of it looked fresh and edible. A lot of the food was well within the use-by date; it was just a bit damaged so it had been thrown away.

> I find it quite exciting now when I'm foraging for food, because you never know what you're going to get...

I find it quite exciting now when I'm foraging for food, because you never know what you're going to get. I never used to cook at home but now I've found that I really enjoy it. Freeganism helps me be a much better cook as I need to come up with new recipes really quickly and to learn which foods will taste good together. I don't want to take too much food and have to throw anything away.

The best thing I ever found was a whole chicken. I made a roast dinner for my family and we used the leftover chicken in a rice dish for dinner the next day. The bones didn't go to waste either as my mum showed me how to make a stock with them for soup! It seems crazy that the chicken was going to be thrown away when we got so much use out of it.

I use supermarkets but you can find food outside cafes, coffee shops, food markets, other food shops and bakeries. The best time to go is at night because that is when the stores have only just thrown out the food so it is still cool and fresh. I usually go in a group of three or four people, not too many so the security guards notice you, but enough people so someone will always be there to help you with bagging the food, giving you a leg up and, crucially, someone to keep a look-out.

The main concerns about freeganism seem to be about the freshness of the food and the legal issues involved. Getting food poisoning really isn't a problem. You just have to be sensible. I have never been ill because I don't eat anything well past the use-by date and try to avoid the fish, shellfish and dairy. The legal issues are a bit more complex. As far as I'm aware, it's not illegal to take property that has been abandoned. However, the law is not clear on these issues and needs to be clarified. If you trespass on private property to get to the bins then you may be prosecuted. However, even on the side of public roads, I have occasionally been chased away by security guards and store owners who don't like people taking the waste food.

> Getting food poisoning really isn't a problem. You just have to be sensible. I have never been ill because I don't eat anything well past the use by date and try to avoid the fish, shellfish and dairy.

Some stores lock their bins and some even pour water or dye on the food to stop people taking it, although I've never come across that. The reasons for this are that the stores don't want any trouble if someone eats something and gets sick, and also because when people who can afford food take it for free, the store misses out on the potential sales. Some stores do donate leftover food to the homeless but I don't think supermarkets will stop wasting food until they are made to by law.

People misunderstand why we're freegans; they think we're just getting food for free because we don't want to pay for it. Freegans are protesting not only against the supermarket system but also about the amount of products and packaging that is wasted every day, which is bad for the environment and of course, adds to the cost of our food. There are ten billion kilos of waste every day in the world, not counting the waste from agriculture and construction. A person living in the West produces around 600 kilos of waste each year, whereas an African living in a city produces only around 150 kilos of waste per year. Getting food for free is a bonus (and as a student it keeps my costs down!). For me, being a freegan is about choosing to be eco-friendly: I recycle, donate old clothes and books to charity and have started growing my own vegetables in my parents' garden. I'll continue to be a freegan for as long as I can because I think it is the right thing to do.

Rhea grew up in Great Yarmouth with her parents and two sisters. She is studying History at the University of East Anglia and dreams of travelling the world and working as a researcher for the British Museum.

The supermarket superpower
by Amelia Wells

I don't boycott supermarkets. I know it's fashionable nowadays to turn up our noses at the capitalist pigs and talk about how beneficial it is to the environment and to local communities to be a locavore (buying only local produce), and I'm not denying that it is, but it's also expensive to constantly be buying free range, organic, locally sourced meat or vegetables hand-grown in the back gardens of Suffolk.

Having said that, I do boycott one supermarket – Tesco. Not a chain, just the one store. It sits on Stokes Croft in Bristol and was the site of local protests. A lobby group of local people led a 'Think Local Boycott Tesco' Campaign there (see www.stokescroft.wordpress.com), arguing that another Tesco store was over-saturation as there are four Tescos within a one mile radius (as well as two Sainsbury's and two Co-ops on the same road). Boycotting the chain is a challenge in itself, since there are so many of them and one is right at that point on the walk to work where you start to wonder if you'll get up the hill without a can of fizz and a sausage roll, especially on hangover days.

> **Ultimately, it doesn't matter if you don't go into a supermarket, thousands of others do.**

Ultimately, it doesn't matter if you don't go into a supermarket, thousands of others do. Not buying a Twix in Tesco won't have much effect, especially not if the area is so saturated that your neighbours can't help but pop in for their milk. In 2010, Tesco had 30.7% of the market in the UK, according to *The Guardian* (Sainsbury's had 16.4%).

The 'consumer choice' we're supposed to have is reduced to 'Tesco, Tesco or Tesco'. And Tesco is taking over the world, quite literally; they buy up chain stores in other countries and insert their brand within. They now have a presence in Thailand, South Korea, Poland, Hungary, Malaysia... and foreign growth is almost certainly the key to their success when sales in Britain are down due to the recession. If they're driving the competition out of business in Turkey, what does it matter if a couple of shops run at a loss in the UK?

But what's the problem with that, anyway? Surely more Tescos means more jobs and a boost to the economy? And isn't that what we're trying to do in this country? Boost the economy? Provide stability for our children? Why aren't you thinking about the future for our children? If you hate Tesco, you hate children! And so the argument goes on. The government seems to think that encouraging big business is the way to boost the economy, as they fail to realise that the economy is a mythical and generally imaginary beast which doesn't comprise of jumbled figures dipping and rising, but ultimately boils down to the time and energy of the population who are actually doing the work. Through this lens, it ought to be obvious that the way to boost the economy is to treat people well, enable them to keep fit, healthy and happy, and thus, in more of a mood to work and be productive. As it is, the economy floats above all of our heads like some kind of dragon which must be satiated with our gold, always threatening to burn down our villages but never really helping us.

In 2008, the Competition Commission completed a major enquiry into the grocery market and found that as more larger stores opened just out of town the number of specialist grocery stores declined, significantly. Are supermarkets going to soak up these out-of-work butchers and bakers and grocers? Or are they going to continue running their stores on minimal staff and keep wages as low as possible? Even if they were able to re-employ these people, it certainly isn't better to go from running your own enterprise to becoming an employee.

So, what's to be done?

The Coalition Government in the UK have, in their business programme, said that they will "seek to ensure a level playing field between small and large retailers by enabling councils to take competition issues into account when drawing up their local plans to shape the direction and type of new retail development." This will then allow local councils and initiatives some say-so in what goes on around their area in terms of new shops.

This is just a minor example of what governments say and what they actually do, so remind them of their responsibilities. Write to your MP, find out if there's a Local Enterprise Partnership in your area and inform local businesses about it. Go to meetings, print out flyers, let people know what's going on and what they can do about it. All the literature flying around Stokes Croft focused on boycotting, and the shop is still there. When the company can afford to run at a loss, they aren't going to care about a few dropped pennies. But when laws and policies are passed and upheld which make it more difficult for corporations to push other businesses out, then things may change.

> We need to believe we can do something about re-invigorating our local area. That's powerful.

We need to believe we can do something about re-invigorating our local area. That's powerful. It's more powerful than walking past Tesco and into Sainsbury's. It's more powerful than putting up stickers or ranting about the whole situation at school. It's actual change. And it may not be easy and it might take a while, but that's why we need to come together as communities, get organised and take that first step forward.

Amelia Wells is currently struggling to make money in the bustling metropolis of London, but hopes one day to have people pay her for writing vitriolic anti-capitalist screeds.

Glossary
by Paul Hannagen

It may be a contradiction, but the essential tip to cooking healthy and cost effectively is to have a well-stocked larder. By this, I mean if you had a few boiled potatoes in the fridge from the Sunday roast and a couple of rashers, combine this with some mayonnaise and wholegrain mustard... maybe a couple of thinly sliced red or spring onions and you have a beautiful potato salad for lunch on Monday!! These little tips are great for not only cooking cost conscious, tasty wholesome food but also for continuing it so you see results both in how you feel and your wallet.

Typically a well-stocked larder should contain any combination of the ingredients listed below. By all means pick up little bits and bobs gradually so it's not too draining on your funds. It is a good project to have as you will see yourself becoming more and more adventurous in your cooking and eating.

Larder

Fine table salt; peppercorns and grinder; Dijon mustard; wholegrain mustard; ketchup; vegetable oil (for cooking); good quality olive oil (for dressing); quality red wine vinegar; quality white wine vinegar; quality balsamic vinegar (for dressings); cheap balsamic (for cooking); paprika; sweet paprika; Star Anise; bay leaves; cloves; fennel seeds; Ras el hanout (Moroccan spice mix); Five spice (Chinese Spice mix); nutmeg; cumin; vanilla essence; cinnamon; chilli powder; fish sauce; oyster sauce; Tabasco; Worcestershire Sauce; soy sauce; sweet chilli sauce; honey; hazelnuts; blanched almonds; mayonnaise. Optional: truffle oil; sherry vinegar; sesame oil; ground nut oil

Quick Fire recipes

All the following recipes serve 4-6 people.
These are a few basic recipes that are great for numerous things, to dress a salad or alternatively garnish a dish. Many freeze well, like the stocks, just take them out the night before and use them in your dish.

Basic Vinaigrette

- 50ml good quality vinegar
- 150ml quality olive oil
- 1 tsp Dijon mustard
- seasoning to taste

Combine all the ingredients in a bowl and whisk together or blitz with a hand blender. You can add a pinch of sugar if you like it less sharp.

The mixture will keep in a covered container for a couple of weeks.

Bechamel sauce

- 500g whole milk
- 30g butter
- 30g flour
- grated nutmeg
- seasoning

Heat the milk in a pan until nearly boiling. Melt the butter in a pan and add the flour. Cook for two minutes until the mixture turns blond. This is called a roux. Add a ladle of milk to the roux at a time until it turns smooth. Continue until all the milk is combined. Season with the nutmeg and seasoning. You can add cheese at this stage for a cheese sauce, or herbs or spices. Place clingfilm against the surface of the sauce so it doesn't form a skin. Place in the fridge and use within two days. Heat with a dash of milk and stir until smooth.

Chicken stock

- 2kgs chicken bones/ carcasses, with skin off, free from your butchers
- 5 carrots
- 2 onions
- 3 cloves garlic
- 1 leek
- 2 sticks of celery
- A sprig of thyme
- A bay leaf
- 5 peppercorns, whole
- A few sprigs of parsley

Put all the ingredients into a large pot and cover with four litres of water. Bring slowly to the boil, skimming off any foam or oil which rises to the top. When the pot comes to a simmer pull to one side so the bubbles run up one side of the pan. This will push all the impurities to one side. Skim off as much as possible. This ensures your stock remains clear and clean tasting. After twenty minutes allow to cook for a further hour and a half. Strain and cool. Use as needed.

The stock also freezes well in containers for up to three months. You can also strain the stock and reduce by half for a more concentrated flavour and to save room in your freezer.

To make veal stock, replace carcasses with chopped veal bones. For beef stock use beef trimmings.

Tomato sauce

- 1 kg tomatoes
- 1 medium onion
- 1 small clove garlic
- 1/4 of a chilli
- 100ml white wine
- sunflower oil
- seasoning

Dice the onion and sweat in the oil for five minutes on a low temperature until translucent. Add the finely chopped chilli and garlic and sweat for a further minute. Add the wine and reduce until dry.
Cut the tomatoes into quarters and add to the pan. Allow to cook for twenty minutes, stirring occasionally. At this stage you can blitz the sauce with a hand-held blender and pass through a sieve for a fine Italian tomato sauce called passata. Leave chunky for more texture or cook for ten minutes less and blitz for a tomato soup... It's up to you!

Red wine sauce

- 5 carrots
- 2 large onions
- 2 cloves of garlic
- 2 sticks celery
- 1 leek
- 1 bottle of red wine
- 2 litres veal or beef stock
- 2 litres chicken stock
- beef trimmings (optional)
- dash of brandy (optional)
- dash of port (optional)
- bay leaf
- sprig of thyme
- sunflower oil
- seasoning

This recipe is very simple despite the list of ingredients. Roughly chop the vegetables and fry in a large pan with the oil until caramelised all over.

Add the beef trimmings if using and recaramelise. Add the port and brandy and recaramelise. Add the bottle of red wine and reduce until syrupy. Add the stocks and bring to a simmer.

Pull off the side of the heat and skim off impurities that come to the top. Repeat until the surface is clear, for about 10 minutes. Add the herbs and reduce until the sauce is reduced and coats the back of a spoon.

Strain through a fine sieve and season to taste.

Serve with grilled or roasted meat or alternatively meaty white fish such as turbot or monkfish.

Kitchen Safety

1. Keep all knives sharp. Surprisingly, if the knife is blunt, you have to add more pressure to cut, this means the knife becomes unstable and is more likely to skew off what you are cutting and into your thumb. Buy some good knives and look after them. The joy of cooking lies in using good quality produce and equipment to channel your inventiveness.

2. Whenever possible, try using different coloured chopping boards for different produce, to avoid cross contamination. Red boards for raw meat, blue for fish and green or brown for fruit and vegetables. These can be picked up quite cheaply from any good culinary shop. If you have a wooden chopping board, wash it, dry it and then, brush it with a scouring pad and some fine table salt. This kills the bacteria in the nooks and crannies of the board and helps eliminate smells.

3. Lastly, be cautious, ovens are hot, pans are heavy and knives are sharp. Never cook when you don't feel up to it and when it comes to food, there is an old mantra in the chef world: **If in doubt throw it out.** Most of all, cooking should be enjoyable, so use these recipes as a reference point and don't be afraid to try something different.

Happy Cooking!!

Paul Hannagen is a young classically French trained chef who has worked in some of the most prestigious restaurants in London. He has just established his own private dining company, Cuisson, which offers private dining and wine events in the London area.

Part 2
Recipes That Don't Cost The Earth

Breakfast On The Go

Breakfast! Morning: the alarm clock goes off. The horror. Every morning. Furry tongue. Bleary eyes. And still, it's time to get up!

Knowing just how hard it is, we've collected a bunch of recipes to spice up your mornings.

Instead of wolfing down half a box of dodgy rainbow-coloured cereal with day-glo orange juice in a plastic bottle, try something new.

We've got a recipe for every occasion. From the mornings when you wake up late and need to leave within five minutes, to those lazy Sundays with friends and family...

And it's always green, easy and healthy... so wake up to your green teen dream...

Banana porridge
by Orso LeCorse

'I love my banana porridge because it has developed my superpowers (strength and speed). I can now help justice to win against evil!!!'

Ingredients

- 1 banana
- 300ml milk
- 1/2 cup porridge oats
- 2 or 3 ice cubes
- a good chunk of chocolate or a nice squeeze of honey

Preparation method

Alright then, peel the banana and put it in a blender (there's no need to chop it up 'cos the blender is going to mash it in a second), add the porridge oats and the milk and the ice if you have it available (if not, it's not going to matter much, but it's nicer if it's cool).

Now you have a choice. If you want it chocolatey add a good chunk according to taste. If you want it choco-intensely-tastic add half a regular sized bar, if you just want a tiny-teency-taste put a thumb sized cube in.

Alternatively, forget the chocolate and add a good squeeze of honey (only you can know the right amount) for a delicious sweet flavour.

Only thing to do now is whack the top of the blender on, give it a good twenty or thirty seconds so that the ice and the chocolate get nice and broken down and then pour into a pint glass. Drink it quick and it's delicious and it'll set you up for the day because those porridge oats have got loads of complex carbohydrate goodness in them.

Just a warning – if you leave it to stand, it'll set and then you're going to need to blend it again. So drink it down and go get to where you gotta be.

Peace!

French Toast
by Nicholas St Meluc

'In France, we call this "pain perdu" which means "lost bread" because we use stale bread to make it. So it's a good recipe to know, because you keep your old bread and turn it into a delicious breakfast!'

Ingredients

- 4 stale bread slices (french bread or toast)
- 1 egg
- 25cl milk
- 30g sugar
- oil

Preparation method

Break the egg in a shallow dish and stir it. In a second shallow dish, pour the milk and the sugar. Mix well to melt the sugar in the milk.

One after the other, dip each slice of bread in the egg for about two minutes on each side.

Every time one of your slices has been dipped long enough in the egg, dip it in the milk and leave it for about the same time, two minutes on each side.

When the first slices are ready, put a little bit of oil in a frying pan, on a medium heat. Cook the slices two at a time. About two minutes on each side or until they get a bit brown and hard. Sprinkle sugar on each side while the slices are cooking. It's ready!

Gruel
by Celine Meuniere

'Gruel is the perfect breakfast for me as it reminds me of my childhood; it reminds me of being a baby even. I find it's a really comforting food, perfect for rainy mornings, or evenings!'

Ingredients

- 500ml milk
- 1 egg
- 1 tbsp flour
- honey

Preparation method

Put the flour in a bowl and slowly add a little bit of cold milk.

Add the egg in order to make a kind of a dough.

Meanwhile, heat the milk. When hot, slowly add it to the mixture, whilst stirring continuously to avoid lumps.

Pour in a pan and boil for a few seconds. Add some honey and eat!

Healthy hash browns
by Felix Kysyl

'I love them because you don't have to cook them individually. You just put everything in the oven and you're done ! And being 'done' without much effort is essential on Sunday mornings...'

Preparation method

Grate the onion and the potatoes (or chop them as finely as possible).

Put the onion and potatoes in a colander and press them down to get all the excess water out. Then transfer the mixture to a bowl.

Finely chop the garlic then add all the ingredients in the bowl together and mix them thoroughly by hand.

Take a baking tray and coat it with a thin layer of butter and then add some flour and spread it so that it sticks to the butter and coats the pan (to stop it sticking to the pan). Tap off any excess flour and add in the mixture, spreading it evenly.

Put the pan in the oven for 20 to 25 minutes at 180°C then put under the grill till the top is crispy and brown.

Now cut into squares and serve them up – hash browns always go well with eggs and bacon and a little ketchup.

Ingredients

- 4 medium potatoes
- 1 onion
- 2 cloves of garlic
- 1 egg
- 1 tsp Worcester-shire sauce
- 1 tbsp oil
- 1 tbsp cornflour
- butter
- salt & pepper

Strawberry yoghurt muesli
by Sonia Gin Fiz

'Waking up in the morning is not an easy task for me. That's why I like breakfasts that are both tasty and easy to make. And I think this one is a very good example...'

Ingredients

- 4 or 5 strawberries
- yoghurt or soy yoghurt
- handful of rice puffs
- handful of oats
- dried bananas
- dried mangos

Preparation method

In a bowl, pour some yoghurt. Wash the strawberries and place them in the bowl too. Then mash them, mixing them with the yoghurt until the yoghurt turns pink.

Add the rice puffs and the oats. Then add the dried mangos and dried bananas...

And that's it! If the strawberries are ripe, you don't even need to add sugar. But if you want a bit of extra sweetness, you can add some honey or agave syrup.

This recipe works well with all kinds of muesli and all kinds of dried fruit. The one I gave you here only happens to be my favourite...

Pancakes
by Leila Varley

'This is a classic, of course, but you can add a little twist by topping it with seasonal fruits, all year round. It usually tastes really good, and it's a perfect way to start the day!'

Preparation method

Place the flour in a big bowl and make a little well in the centre. Crack the eggs in the well and start whisking to mix them in. Add the oil.

Then start pouring the milk very slowly, in small quantities. Every time you pour a bit more, you should keep stirring to mix all the liquid into the flour and avoid lumps.

When the batter is liquid enough, pour in the rest of the milk. You should have a rather thick batter.

Some say you should leave the batter to rest for half an hour, but I personally don't do that. It doesn't seem to make much difference.

Heat up a pan on moderate heat and wipe it using a tissue with oil on it. When it's hot, pour in some of the batter. You can make very thin or very thick pancakes, it's up to you. But if the mixture is thicker, then it will take longer to cook.

A thin pancake should take about thirty seconds to cook on each side. When it's ready take it off the heat and add whatever you like. My favourite is lemon juice and sugar, but I also really like pineapple pancakes!

Ingredients

- 100 g plain flour
- 2 eggs
- 300 ml semi-skimmed milk
- 1 tbsp oil
- a pinch of salt

Liver salad and eggs
by Taliani Dorina Nixon

'This is a Jewish recipe, from Eastern Europe. It's my grandmother's recipe and I consider it to be part of my heritage. I find it good in the morning, because it's a strong flavour and at least it wakes you up!'

Ingredients

- 500g chicken liver
- 6 eggs
- 2 onions
- 2 spring onions
- 1 tsp cumin
- chopped parsley
- salt & pepper

Preparation method

Clean the livers and cut off the venous parts. Boil the eggs for ten minutes. Remove them from the pan and leave them in cold water.

In a pan, colour the onions in one tablespoon of olive oil. Add the livers and let them set on high heat while stirring.

Shell the eggs and mash them with a fork into a very thin semolina. Add salt, pepper, chopped parsley and the chopped spring onions.

Check that the livers are cooked: open one, it should be brown, and not pink. Remove the livers from the heat and mash them with a fork. Add salt, pepper, cumin and chopped parsley.

Put the two preparations into two separate bowls. You can also blend them together, but it is nicer to have two colours. Decorate with parsley branches, and serve cool. Traditionally, it is eaten together.

Lunch Munch

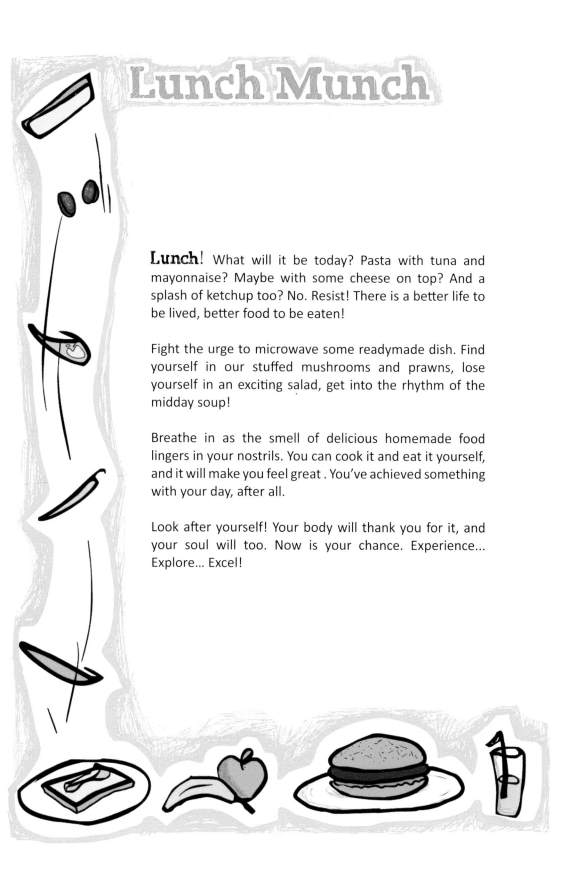

Lunch! What will it be today? Pasta with tuna and mayonnaise? Maybe with some cheese on top? And a splash of ketchup too? No. Resist! There is a better life to be lived, better food to be eaten!

Fight the urge to microwave some readymade dish. Find yourself in our stuffed mushrooms and prawns, lose yourself in an exciting salad, get into the rhythm of the midday soup!

Breathe in as the smell of delicious homemade food lingers in your nostrils. You can cook it and eat it yourself, and it will make you feel great . You've achieved something with your day, after all.

Look after yourself! Your body will thank you for it, and your soul will too. Now is your chance. Experience... Explore... Excel!

Luncheon stuffed mushrooms
by Kim Simpson

'I love cooking stuffed mushrooms because they don't require too much preparation. They are a good way to use up any old bits of veg you have lying around, and because they're great on their own for lunch or a snack, or on the side with dinner.'

Preparation method

To prepare the large portobello mushrooms, wash and remove the stalks then rub with olive oil before placing on a baking tray.

Melt a knob of butter in a pan over a medium heat.

Ingredients *serves 2*

- 2 portobello mushrooms
- ½ courgette
- 6 closed cup mushrooms
- ½ red pepper
- ¼ aubergine
- ¼ tin chopped tomatoes
- 2 cloves garlic
- ½ onion
- ¼ cup oats
- dash of double cream (optional)
- 2 rashers of smoked back bacon (optional)
- grated cheese of your choice (mature cheddar or stilton both work well)

Wash and chop all of your other vegetables (except the tomatoes) into small cubes and add to the pan.

Add the bacon, sliced into small squares, if you want a non-vegetarian meal. Season with salt, pepper and other herbs of your choice.

Heat for five to seven minutes or until cooked and mushy, stirring regularly. Add the oats, the chopped tomatoes, and for a richer taste, a dash of double cream. Once the filling is made, spoon it into the Portobello mushrooms, and top with cheese.

Put the stuffed mushrooms into a pre-heated oven 180°C for ten minutes.

Any filling that's left over is great on toast, or liquidised for soup.

Honey prawns with chilli and rosemary
by Edward Gosling

'It's really easy to change the amounts in this recipe, depending on how many people you're cooking for. Once you've cooked it once or twice, throw out all my measurements and just add according to what you like, a big glug of oil, a generous pour of honey...'

Preparation method

Put the prawns in a mixing bowl. Peel and chop the garlic, deseed the chilli (because you want the heat and flavour of the chilli rather than something that will blow your head off) chop it up, run your fingers down the sprig of rosemary so you get off all the little leaves, pop them all in the bowl and add some salt and freshly ground black pepper. Add the honey and the olive oil.

Next cut two circles of bread per person and put them on the plate. Take the seasonal greens and put them in the centre of the plate. Optionally, chop up an avocado to add.

Take your mixing bowl full of ingredients, stir it round and then pour the whole thing into a wok on high heat. Now watch it sizzle and bubble and get really tasty. It only takes about five minutes. As soon as the prawns turn pink all the way through, it's done.

Serve an equal amount of prawns per person and then drizzle all the delicious honey, chilli, garlic, rosemary and oil over the greens and the bread.

Last thing to do is squeeze a little lemon on the top.

Ingredients
serves 4

• 24 uncooked big prawns or 4 handfuls uncooked small ones
• 4 cloves garlic, finely chopped
• 1 decent sized chilli, finely chopped
• 4-5 sprigs rosemary
• 6 tbsp honey (good quality, lavender or orange blossom)
• 4 tbsp virgin olive oil (a really good one)
• 1 baguette
• 1 bag of seasonal greens (eg spinach, rocket and watercress)
• 1 lemon (optional)
• 1 avocado (optional)
• salt & pepper

Japanish soup
by Sarah Duvelier

'This soup is inspired by Japanese food. I invented it because I wanted to make something Asian with an exotic twist to it, and even if it's not properly Japanese, it tastes delicious and it's really easy to make!'

Preparation method

Boil a big pan of water. Slice the mushrooms and put them in the boiling water with the sugar snaps. Chop the asparagus in three to four cm pieces. Five minutes later, add the asparagus and cook for six more minutes. Add the miso soup paste and stir to dilute; you can also add some more soy sauce, if you like. Add the ginger. You want the asparagus to be a bit crunchy. Add salt to taste.

Meanwhile, chop the tofu in thick pieces and put it on a low heat in a frying pan with sesame oil. Sprinkle with sesame seeds.

Add a generous amount of soy sauce. The tofu has to get brownish but you need to cook it on both sides and turn it over to prevent it from burning.

When the vegetables are nearly ready, add the rice noodle pasta and two minutes later, add the beansprouts.

Take off the heat.

Serve the soup in a bowl.

Add the tofu on top, and sprinkle with the chopped spring onion.

It's ready!

Ingredients
serves 4

- 300g rice noodles
- 400g tofu
- 250g asparagus
- 250g portobello mushrooms
- 150g sugar snaps
- 30g ginger
- 4 tbsp miso soup paste
- sesame oil
- sesame seeds
- soy sauce
- 2 spring onions
- salt & pepper

Green and hearty smoked mackerel salad
by Andy Gold

'I make this in my packed lunch box. I keep olive oil and salt and pepper in a drawer in my desk and I just pop the lemon in the bag to take with me after I've zested it. Then I slice it and squeeze the juice through my fingers (to filter out the pips).'

Preparation method

Sweat the red onion in olive oil, grate in some lemon zest. Add your bulgar wheat (or quinoa), a pinch of salt and water (usually twice as much as the wheat) and cook according to pack instructions.

Allow to cool. Mix the wheat and the leaves. Remove the skin from your mackerel fillets and the brown 'vein' running down the middle of the skin side. Break into generous pieces and arrange over leaves.

At work: Season well with olive oil, lemon juice and salt and pepper. Eat!

Ingredients
serves 1

- 2 smoked mackerel fillets
- 75g bulgar wheat, or quinoa
- 2 handfuls of a mix of rocket, spinach and /or watercress
- red onion
- lemon
- olive oil
- salt & pepper

Mediterranean couscous with roasted vegetables
by Sam Well

'Couscous is pretty bland and unexciting on its own, but it works like a flavour sponge – so all you need to do is give it a load of big exciting ingredients for it to soak up and then sit back and watch it transform into something fantastic!'

Preparation method

Roughly chop the onions, peppers, courgette, tomatoes and parsley; finely chop the garlic and put them all in a large roasting tray with a good splash of olive oil and balsamic vinegar. Sprinkle over some salt and pepper and mix it all together with your hands. Put the tray in the oven for twenty-five to thirty minutes at 200°C. Half way through cooking take out the pan and shake it about a bit.

Chop up the olives and artichoke hearts and pop them in a large mixing bowl with the juice from the lemon. When the vegetables are roasted, add them to the bowl – making sure you really scrape the bottom of the tray well because that's where some of the tastiest caramelised bits are. Add the couscous and mix it all together.

Add enough boiling water to cover it all. Put a lid on the bowl and leave for five minutes.

Now see if it's ready. If there's still some water left in the mixture try just stirring it for a second so the water has a chance to get to all of the couscous. If it looks a little dry add a touch more boiling water and leave it for a minute. When this is done, chop up the feta into loose chunks and add them, mixing them together but being careful not to break them up too much. Serve with some lettuce in a very light dressing – and enjoy.

Ingredients *serves 6*

- 2 red onions
- 2 red or yellow peppers
- 1 large courgette
- 4 medium tomatoes (or a bunch of little cherry ones)
- 1 handful of fresh parsley
- 1 lemon
- 4 cloves garlic
- 1 handful olives
- 1 handful artichoke hearts
- 200g feta cheese
- 2 cups couscous
- olive oil
- balsamic vinegar
- salt & pepper

Chicken with ginger and broccoli
by Dong Tran

'I used to love this Vietnamese dish when my mum cooked it for me as a child. I started cooking it myself when I began living on my own. It's cheap and simple to make and can be stored for up to two days.'

Preparation method

Place a saucepan on a medium heat and add all the chicken and the ginger. Gently cook, turning the pieces around from time to time. Add salt and pepper.

Crumble the chicken stock cube on top then pour in some boiling water until the chicken is just covered.

Put the heat on the lowest setting and leave to simmer for twenty to thirty minutes with the lid on. Keep checking the pan so that it doesn't dry out. If it looks a bit dry then add some more water.

Just before serving, add the broccoli and cover with the lid again for two minutes.
Serve with boiled rice.

Ingredients
serves 4

• 4 chicken legs with skin (thighs and drumsticks)
• 1 cube of chicken stock
• 5cm piece of ginger, finely chopped
• 1 head of broccoli (cut into pieces)
• salt & pepper

Salad of seasonal greens, with toasted seeds, beans and feta cheese
by Sarah Veniard

'For the seasonal leaves, fresh from the garden is best, so get growing in your garden or window box!'

Ingredients　　serves 4

• a selection of tasty seasonal leaves, such as chard, rocket, mizuna and sorrel
• 2 small handfuls toasted seeds (such as sesame, sunflower, flax)
• 1 tin flageolet beans
• half a block of feta cheese
• 2 tbsp extra virgin olive oil
• 2 tbsp balsamic vinegar
• juice of 1 lemon
• 1 tsp mustard
• salt & pepper

Preparation method

Wash the leaves and place them in a large salad bowl. Gently mix in the beans.

Crumble the feta cheese into the bowl.

Sprinkle a couple of handfuls of toasted seeds over the salad.

Whisk together the olive oil, balsamic vinegar, lemon juice and mustard.

Season with salt and pepper. Mix and serve for a sparkling summertime treat!

Flower prawn soup
by Emma Ogoe

'I called this dish 'Flower Prawn Soup' because when you cut and cook the prawns they look like little flowers. This recipe is influenced by a kind of Korean fast food called "Kumchi". It tastes amazing!'

Preparation method

Boil one litre of water in a saucepan. Chop the tomato, onions, garlic and lemongrass. Add them to the boiling water. Boil for two to three minutes. If you want to make it hotter, chop the chilli and add to your taste. Chop the mushrooms (not too finely). Add these to the mixture.

Add the peas, cook for a further three minutes. Put in the noodles and add the sachet that comes with them. Take the king prawns one, by one, and cut an incision so that they open up like a flower when cooked. Add into the mixture and cook for two to three minutes.

To present, use a soup bowl and twist the noodles around a fork or with tongs, remove from the liquid and put in a pile in the bowl. Then add the liquid so that the prawns are floating around the noodles with the vegetables and prawns.

Ingredients *serves 4*

- 1 clove of garlic
- 1 stalk of lemongrass
- 4 packets of prawn flavoured instant noodles
- 1 fresh tomato
- 1 onion
- ¼ of a Scotch Bonnet Chilli (optional)
- 1 handful of peas
- 1 handful of mushrooms
- 1 small packet of fresh raw king prawns (you can use frozen but make sure they are fully defrosted before you cook)
- salt & pepper

Rib it up!
by Charles Aston

'I picked this recipe because it's a tastebud thriller but doesn't blow the budget or require much effort.'

Ingredients *serves 4*

• ½ rack of pork ribs (ask your butcher to cut into 4 portions)
• 1 can of chopped tomatoes
• 1 large red onion
• 1 stick of celery
• 1 carrot
• 1 small red chilli, finely chopped (remove the seeds if you don't like your food too spicy)
• 1 beef stock cube
• 2 tsp vegetable bouillon
• 1 bag of new potatoes
• a good handful of parsley, finely chopped
• 1 tbsp oil
• salt & pepper

Preparation method

Finely chop all the vegetables. On a high heat, fry the oil in a large saucepan. Add the rack of ribs and colour for two minutes. Lower the heat and add the vegetables and chilli. Sweat for approximately ten minutes until soft.

Crumble the stock cube and bouillon on top of the mix, stir, then add the can of chopped tomatoes. Simmer on a low heat for a minimum of forty-five minutes with the lid on. The longer you cook it, the tenderer the meat will be but don't let it boil dry.

Meanwhile, cook the new potatoes in a pan of salted boiling water until soft. Drain and put back in the pan. Stir in the parsley and a little butter then crush the potatoes with a fork. Season with salt and pepper.

Put a spoonful of the crushed parsley potatoes in the middle of each plate and place the ribs (still on the bone) on top. Pour some of the sauce over the top and serve.

Roast squash salad
by Alex Manunza

'The chilli oil mix keeps really well so you can always just have a pot of this in your drawer at work or make one and bring in with you, or wherever. This recipe works especially well with red mustard salad leaves, but you can use any kind of salad, it will still be really good.'

Preparation method

Pre-heat your oven to 200°C. Chop up the squash in big chunks and place on a baking tray. Put in the oven and roast.

When you can insert the blade of a knife easily in the squash, it's cooked.

Put roast squash, parma ham and the red mustard salad, salt and pepper in a container.

Wrap crusty bread in clingfilm or buy fresh on your way in to work. Prepare a small bowl of olive oil with chopped chillies into it .

Take to work and mix it together when ready to eat.

Ingredients   *serves 1*

- 2 large handfuls of chunky pieces of roast squash
- 2 slices of parma ham
- Handful of red mustard salad leaves, lettuce or else
- 1 slice of crusty bread
- olive oil
- chillies

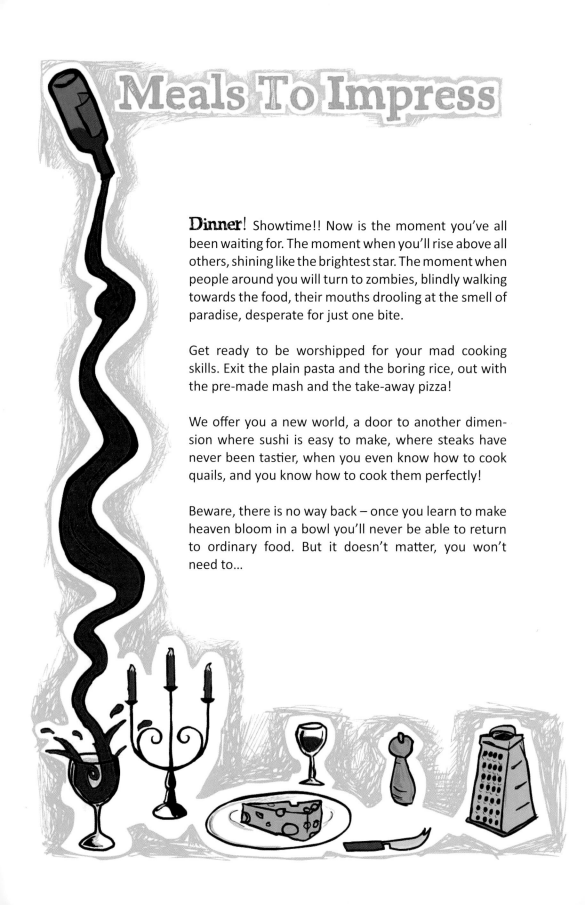

Meals To Impress

Dinner! Showtime!! Now is the moment you've all been waiting for. The moment when you'll rise above all others, shining like the brightest star. The moment when people around you will turn to zombies, blindly walking towards the food, their mouths drooling at the smell of paradise, desperate for just one bite.

Get ready to be worshipped for your mad cooking skills. Exit the plain pasta and the boring rice, out with the pre-made mash and the take-away pizza!

We offer you a new world, a door to another dimension where sushi is easy to make, where steaks have never been tastier, when you even know how to cook quails, and you know how to cook them perfectly!

Beware, there is no way back – once you learn to make heaven bloom in a bowl you'll never be able to return to ordinary food. But it doesn't matter, you won't need to...

Olly's smokey meat feast
by Oliver Quelch

'This recipe is a Spanish take on a Bolognese; a smokey twist on a well known classic. It's especially good as a winter warmer.'

Preparation method

Heat the olive oil in a saucepan. Add the chopped chorizo and fry until the oil has been released and the chorizo is crispy.

Add the minced beef and fry until brown. Remove the meat from the pan by straining in a sieve and set aside.

Fry the chopped onion, celery, carrot and garlic on a low heat for ten minutes, until soft and lightly-coloured.

Put the meat back into the saucepan and add the cherry tomatoes and tomato purée.

Bring to the boil and simmer for one and a half hours. Serve with spaghetti or tagliatelle.

Ingredients   *serves 4*

- 450g minced beef
- 100g chorizo, chopped
- 10g tomato purée
- 1 carrot
- 1 stick of celery
- 1 tbsp olive oil
- ½ tsp paprika (optional)
- 200ml beef stock
- 1 red onion, chopped
- 1 clove of garlic
- 2 x 400g tins of cherry tomatoes
- 1 lemon
- salt & pepper

Sizzling steak with mashed potatoes
by Alaine Lemaire

'No one says no to a steak. A lot of young people think that steak is expensive and is difficult to cook but I wanted to show that it is a simple thing to make but still delicious.'

Ingredients
serves 4

- 4 rib eye steaks
- 1kg bag of King Edward potatoes
- 2 tbsp malt vinegar
- 2 tbsp butter
- 500g frozen peas
- ½ cup double cream
- 2 tbsp sunflower oil
- salt & pepper

Preparation method

Season the steaks with the salt, pepper and vinegar. Cover with clingfilm and put in the fridge.

Peel your potatoes, rinse and cut into halves then put in a pan and cover with boiling water. Add salt to the water and leave to boil for twenty minutes until soft.

Drain then mash the potatoes and put back on a low heat, stirring continuously. Mix in the butter then the double cream. Season to taste and put to the side with the lid on so it keeps warm.

Boil the frozen peas for five minutes then drain. Meanwhile, heat a frying pan on a high heat. When it starts to smoke, lower the heat and add the sunflower oil.

Fry the steaks for a minute on each side (a little longer if you like your steak well done).

Serve with the mashed potatoes and peas, pouring the juice from the steak on top.

Roasted fillet of salmon with hollandaise sauce
by Lola de Courroux

'To me this is real cooking, you've got four elements here that compliment each other: the lemon is going to bring together the fish and the sauce and the garlic will make the spinach and the potatoes sing. Happy eating!'

Preparation method

Boil the potatoes for fifteen minutes. Heat oven to 180°C and put a roasting tray with a good splash of oil in it.

Place each salmon fillet in the middle of a tinfoil square and squeeze 1/4 of a lemon over it. Sprinkle the dried dill tops then sprinkle with salt and black pepper. Wrap the fillets in the tinfoil. Put them side by side on a tray.

Roughly chop four cloves of garlic and a handful of fresh thyme. When your potatoes are boiled, drain them and place them on the hot tray. Add the garlic, the thyme and a good sprinkle of salt and pepper. Roll the potatoes around in the oil then pop the tray in the top of the oven and put the salmon in at the same time in the middle of the oven. They will take twenty minutes each. After ten minutes, take out the potatoes and roll them around in the oil again so they cook equally on all sides.

Steam the spinach so that it wilts down. Put a knob of butter into a frying pan, fry two cloves of garlic for a minute and then add the spinach before turning it down to a very low heat. Leave for a few minutes.

For the sauce: put the egg yolks into a mixing bowl. Add salt and black pepper. Whisk hard for about a minute. Heat up the juice of half a lemon with the white wine vinegar till it starts to foam. Gently add it to the egg yolks while whisking hard. Next, melt the butter and add it slowly to the egg yolks while whisking. Keep whisking for another thirty seconds. Pour sauce over fish and serve.

Ingredients   *serves 4*

- 4 salmon fillets
- 1-2 lemons
- 6 cloves of garlic
- dried dill tops
- 20-25 new potatoes
- fresh thyme
- 450g fresh spinach
- 2 eggs
- 1-2 tbsp white wine vinegar
- 110g of butter / vegetable fat
- salt
- freshly ground black pepper

Risotto with rocket salad pesto
by Beth Gilliams

'This is my father's recipe, it's one of his favourites. He taught me how to do it when I was a child and now I keep doing it all the time because it is so simple, and at the same time so sophisticated!'

Preparation method

For the pesto:
Peel the garlic and chop up the parmesan. Blend the rocket with the garlic, the parmesan and some basil leaves.

Progressively add the oil, and a little water if necessary.

For the risotto:
Grate the parmesan and keep some of it to decorate the risotto at the end. Cut the butter into cubes.

Boil the water and add the stock. Finely chop up the onion.

In a pan, heat up one teaspoon of olive oil and sweat the onion. Add the rice and stir on medium heat until the grains turn transparent (approx. three minutes).

Add the white wine and stir until absorbed. Add a ladle of stock and let the rice absorb it slowly. Repeat until all the stock is added. Always turn the spoon in the same direction to avoid 'breaking' the preparation.

Add the butter and finally the pesto (which must not cook!).

Serve immediately with grated parmesan.

Ingredients *serves 2*

- 125 g risotto rice
- 1 chicken stock
- 1/2 litre water
- 10 cl dry white wine
- 50 g parmesan
- 1 tbsp olive oil
- 30g butter
- 1/2 onion (chopped)
- salt & pepper

pesto
- 35 g rocket salad
- 1/2 garlic clove
- a few basil leaves
- 2 tbsp olive oil
- 35 g chopped parmesan

Jai's killer quail
by Jai Harrower

'This recipe is based on one I was taught in a cooking demonstration. The original version used chicken but I've adapted it to suit my palate. It tastes delicious and is relatively easy to make. The trick is not to overcook the quail!'

Ingredients *serves 2*

- 2 quail (ask your butcher to spatchcock it)
- 2 bunches of cherry tomatoes on the vine
- 2 King Edwards or other big potatoes
- 1 packet of purple sprouting broccoli
- 3 cloves of garlic, chopped and 1 clove of garlic, crushed
- 2 sprigs of thyme
- 1 sprig of rosemary
- 4 sage leaves
- good olive oil
- a knob of unsalted butter,
- salt & pepper

Preparation method

Pre-heat the oven to 180°C. Chop the sage and half the thyme and mix with the butter. Rub a little olive oil, salt and pepper and the crushed garlic clove onto the quail. Leave both the butter and the quail in the fridge for twenty minutes.

Wash and scrub the potatoes. Cut into one cm thick slices leaving the skin on. Place onto a greaseproof tray with the remaining thyme, garlic, olive oil, salt and pepper. Put into the oven.

Heat a tablespoon of oil in a pan. When hot, place the quail skin side down and cook for around eight minutes until the skin starts to crisp. Place into the oven with the tomatoes alongside it. Cook for five minutes, turn over the quail and cook for another five minutes until the meat is cooked through – pierce it with a knife to check it's juicy but not pink.

Cook the broccoli in boiling water, strain and then add a knob of the herb butter to glaze them up.

Place your potatoes onto the plate, then the broccoli then the quail, finished with the tomatoes and a drizzle of olive oil.

Spaghetti alla Puttanesca
by Scott Mattock

'This is a cheap and easy dish to create, using mainly store cupboard ingredients – go try!!'

Preparation method

Put the anchovies in a frying pan along with the oil from the tinned tuna (if using – if not, add four to five tablespoons of olive oil).

Put the pan on a medium heat and let the anchovies dissolve into the oil. Once done, add the garlic and chilli and fry gently for two minutes.

Add the olives and capers and fry for a further minute. Add chopped parsley stalks then add the cherry tomatoes. Simmer on a medium to low heat for around twelve minutes to allow the flavours to blend. If you are using tuna, add it into the sauce and simmer for a further three minutes. Add the chopped parsley and basil to taste. Squeeze half a lemon on top and season if needed.

Before serving, mix in some cooked spaghetti as well as a little of the water the spaghetti was cooked in. Serve with warm bread.

Ingredients   serves 2

- 8 anchovies
- 1 clove of garlic (finely sliced)
- 1 tsp chilli flakes
- 2 handfuls of black olives (sliced in half)
- 1 tbsp capers (in brine)
- handful of parsley and basil
- 1 can of cherry tomatoes
- 1 lemon
- 1 can of tuna in olive oil (optional)
- spaghetti
- salt & pepper

Chicken chorizo casserole
by Charles Patterson

'This is a good meal to cook when you have friends around because it's easy to make huge quantities of it and it usually pleases everyone. A good Saturday night meal.'

Preparation method

Chicken chorizo:
Fry the garlic and basil for thirty seconds. Add the onion and soften till golden-brown. Add the chicken and cook till sealed. Add the peppers and chorizo and cook for one to two minutes. Add the tinned tomatoes, half a glass of wine, salt and pepper, and leave to cook for thirty minutes.

Ingredients *serves 6*

Casserole:
• 4 chicken breasts (rough cut)
• 2 chorizo sausages (sliced)
• 1 onion (diced)
• 4 cloves of garlic
• 2 red peppers
• 1 yellow pepper
• handful of basil leaves, (torn)
• 2 tins of tomatoes (chopped)
• white wine
• salt, pepper, olive oil

Roasted tomatoes:
• 10 large tomatoes halved
• thyme
• 5 cloves of garlic halved
• salt, pepper, olive oil

Roasted new potatoes:
• new potatoes
• garlic
• thyme
• vegetable oil
• salt & pepper

Roasted tomatoes:
Pre-heat oven to 180-200°C. Place the halved-tomatoes cut-side up on a large roasting tray. Put half a clove of garlic on each. Drizzle with olive oil, season with salt and pepper, and add thyme on top.

Cook for thirty to forty minutes, or until lightly charred.

Roasted new potatoes:
Parboil the potatoes for five minutes until soft.

Drain, cover in oil, season with salt, pepper and a sprig of thyme and cook for thirty to forty minutes in a roasting tray.

Sushi for dummies
by Pauline Blistene

'I was taught how to make sushi whilst travelling in Japan at the age of fourteen. If you're not too picky about how traditionally made they are, it's a great thing to make because it impresses everyone, and it's actually quite easy once you get used to it.'

Ingredients   *serves 8*

- 1kg sushi rice
- 1 avocado
- 3 medium sized carrots
- 100g green beans (optional)
- 1 cucumber
- 190g cooked king prawns
- 250g raw tuna
- 250g raw salmon
- 10 tbsp rice vinegar
- 5 tbsp sugar
- 4 tblsp sesame seeds
- around 8 seaweed sheets
- 1 sushi mat
- 1 tsp salt
- pickled ginger, wasabi, soya sauce to taste

Preparation method

Put the rice in a large saucepan, cover with water and rinse two or three times. Add one and a half litres of water and bring to the boil on a low to medium heat.

Meanwhile, start chopping the vegetables lengthways (the longer and thinner the strips are, the better). Also, chop the fish lengthways but keep some square bits to make those little balls of rice with fish on them. To be really honest, there is a proper Japanese way to cut the fish, which makes the sushi even better. But that's quite an advanced thing to do, and I find that even if you don't cut the fish as a specialist would do, it still works...

Mix the vinegar, the sugar and the salt and put on a medium heat until it all melts. When the rice has absorbed all the water, take off the heat and add the vinegary solution. Mix well and cover with a cloth.

Let it cool down. Then separate the rice in two bowls. In one of the bowls, add the sesame seeds and stir. Take a seaweed sheet and place it on the sushi mat, making sure that the bright side of the sheet is facing the mat. Then, start spreading rice on the sheet. I find it easier to do this with the back of a spoon rather than with the spoon itself. Try to spread the rice evenly, but stop a few centimetres before you reach the end of the sheet.

When your rice is evenly spread, add some vegetables and some fish. Lay them lengthwise. One strip of cucumber, one strip of fish, one of carrot and a little bit of avocado is a standard for me. But of course you can put pretty much anything you like in sushi, and you can try

different things too! You can make different sized sushi rolls, depending on whether you want each roll to be filled with a lot of things or whether you want them lighter. When your vegetables and your fish are all placed on the sheet, you're ready to roll.

Dip the tips of your fingers in a little bit of water and spread it on the seaweed sheet, where there's no rice. Roll the mat forward, making sure you are pressing the rice and all the vegetables and fish between your fingers. When the mat is doing a loop, try and pull its end upwards in order to keep rolling the seaweed, but not the mat itself.

Keep rolling the sushi roll and when you finish, keep squeezing it in the sushi mat for a few seconds. Also, make sure that the end of the seaweed sheet sticks to itself, as it is what will keep the roll together.

When your roll is ready, it should be firm on both ends. It is now time to take a very sharp knife and be very careful. Pour water on your knife and start carefully slicing the roll. You can get rid of the ends of the roll, which are never very nice.

Try to make even slices, cleaning your knife and making it wet again every time you finish a roll.

If you have fish and rice left, you can make small balls of rice, squeezing them very firmly, and then place a square piece of fish on top of it.

When all your rolls are ready, place them on a plate with some pickled ginger, soya sauce and wasabi.

It's ready! And it's delicious...

Green pesto tagliatelle
by Jack Wells

'This dish is cheap, easy and filling. It's my mum's recipe and I think she's the best chef in the world.'

Preparation method

In a blender, whiz together the basil, pine nuts, cheese, salt, pepper and one clove of garlic.

Pour in the olive oil until your pesto sauce has reached a desired consistency (it should be like a wet, but not runny, paste).

Cut the bacon into squares and slice the mushrooms. Fill a saucepan with boiled water and add the tagliatelle.

Meanwhile, fry off the bacon, mushrooms and crushed garlic until coloured.

Drain the pasta when soft and pour it back into the saucepan.

Next add the bacon, garlic and mushrooms to the pasta.

Then add the cream and pesto sauce and heat it all through.

Serve with bread.

Ingredients *serves 4*

- 1 big handful of basil
- 30g pine nuts
- 8 rashers of bacon
- 12 button mushrooms
- 2 cloves of garlic
- olive oil
- tagliatelle
- 30g parmesan, Pecorino or Grana Padano cheese
- 1 splash of cream (quantity depends on how creamy you want it)
- salt & pepper

Tapas For Parties

Celebration! There you are, alone in the kitchen, a party to prepare. The saucepans are taunting you, the hob is mocking you, and even worse, all those plates are so empty they could make you cry... A sad old packet of crisps is your only ally.

You've got a crowd of people coming over and you know you won't be able to stop them from arguing when the crisps run out ... so how do you feed them? Keep them happy?

No worries. Chill! What could make anyone happier than some aubergine caviar and a mini pizza? Or some tortillas, marinated peppers, tapenade and salsa! There will be a party. Even better, a tasty, healthy green, extraordinary party! Because that's how good you are...

Tapenade on bread
by Matan Yaniv

'I learnt to make tapenade whilst I was travelling in France, around the age of fifteen. It's simple to make and it's also quite impressive for those who don't know it. Now I'm back in Israel, I do it all the time.'

Ingredients

- 50g caper
- 300g olives (black, green or both)
- 1 clove of garlic
- 1 tbsp lemon juice
- 10cl olive oil
- bread

Preparation method

Mince the capers finely with 50g of olives, the lemon juice and the clove of garlic in a mortar (or with a food processor).

Add the 250g of remaining olives and grind, but not too much so that small bits of olive remain.

When the ingredients are evenly mixed, add the oil progressively until you obtain a smooth paste, not too thick.

Spread the tapenade on small pieces of bread and lay on a plate to present to your guests!

Broad beans with pancetta and chardonnay vinegar
by Paul Hannagen

'This is an easy recipe, however, with all easy recipes the secret lies in the execution both of cooking and seasoning. This is what the Spanish traditionally call "tapas"...'

Ingredients

- 500 g frozen broad beans
- 100 g pancetta (smoked pork belly) or thick cut smoked streaky bacon
- 50 g butter
- good quality olive oil
- pepper
- good quality Chardonnay vinegar

Preparation method

Put a large pan of water on the boil. While it is heating, slice your bacon into lardons (thicker than a match stick).

Put a frying pan on the heat and add the butter. When the butter starts to foam, add the bacon. Stir continuously for three to five minutes until the bacon is caramelized all over, taking care not to burn the butter. Take off the heat and keep to one side.

Meanwhile, add salt to the boiling water until it tastes like seawater. Add the broad beans and cook for four minutes. After four minutes, strain and add to ice-cold water.

When fully chilled, pop the broad beans from the pods taking care not to crush them.

Put the frying pan back on the heat until the pan starts to sizzle. Add the broad beans. Cook for one minute or until warmed through.

Take off the heat and mix through olive oil vinegar and pepper to taste.

Serve in a tapas dish.

Aubergine caviar on garlic bread
by Hannah Well

'Aubergine caviar is delicious, but it's even better if you spread it on garlic bread: just rub some garlic on pieces of bread, add a touch of olive oil, and toast in the oven for a few minutes. Then spread the aubergine paste on it when it's still warm. Yuuumiiii!'

Ingredients

- 2 large aubergines
- 10cl olive oil
- 6 cloves of garlic
- 1 tbsp lemon juice
- salt & pepper

Preparation method

Pre-heat the oven to 200°C.

Remove the green ends of the aubergine and cut them in halves. With a knife, make several incisions into the flesh, and insert pieces of garlic inside.

Pour a dash of olive oil on them and put in the oven, skin downside for forty to fifty minutes (the aubergines must be entirely cooked).

Remove the flesh with a spoon and mix it in the food processor with olive oil, salt and pepper. Let it cool down before spreading on warm garlic bread.

Spanish tortilla
by Mike Silver Junior

'This is a classic recipe which is so simple despite the list of ingredients. Change the filling to whatever you want, by all means. The only thing which must remain constant is the ratio of egg, onion and potato... the rest is up to you!'

Ingredients

- 10 eggs
- 2 large potatoes
- 2 medium onions
- basil
- 2 roasted red peppers (skins taken off)
- 2 tomatoes
- 3 chorizo dolce (preferrably Brindisa)
- sunflower oil
- seasoning

Preparation method

First peel the onions, slice in half, take out the root and slice very thinly. Add to a pan with a splash of oil and season. Place on the lowest heat possible and sweat, watching that the onions don't stick, until golden brown, soft and cooked through.

Peel the potatoes and slice into one cm thick rounds. Place on a roasting tray with oil seasoning and roast at 180°C until cooked through and golden brown (but not too crisp).

Slice up the tomatoes and peppers and season. When the potatoes and onions are done, place a frying pan on the heat. Dice the chorizo and add to the pan. Fry until lightly coloured.

Beat the ten eggs in a bowl with some seasoning. Add the cooked potato and the rest of the ingredients and stir to incorporate all the ingredients. Place in the oven at 180°C and cook for between sixteen to twenty minutes .

Turn halfway through to ensure even cooking. Take out of the oven and cool. When cool turn out onto a plate and serve.

Instant mini pizzas
by Felix Louis Bertrand

'These mini pizzas are perfect when you have friends over because they are really easy and quick to make. When you make a big pizza and have some dough left over, it's also a good way to use it.'

Ingredients

- 100 g flour
- 1/2 tsp salt
- 1 pinch of baking powder
- 1 egg
- 2 tbsp olive oil
- tomato purée
- balsamic vinegar
- ground almonds
- 1 tomato
- pumpkin seeds
- rosemary

Preparation method

Mix the flour, salt and baking powder in a large bowl. Add the egg and the oil, and mix well. Add water progressively: there is enough when you can form a ball that does not stick to your fingers.

Make small balls of dough and flatten them with your fingers. Shape them like small pizzas and place them on baking paper.

Pre-heat your oven to 170°C. In a bowl, mix tomato purée, ground almonds, balsamic vinegar, salt and pepper. There are no right or wrong quantities, it's all about the way you want it to taste, so just make sure you make a thick paste.

Spread the mixture on your small pizzas and add chopped tomato. You can finish off by adding some pumpkin seeds and rosemary on top.
Put in the oven and cook for five to ten minutes.

Mackerel on crostini
by Jahni Lake

'If you don't fancy making crostini, this works well on crackers, sliced French bread or rice cakes.'

Ingredients

- 2 mackerel fillets
- sour cream
- dill
- chives
- chilli
- french bread
- oil
- salt

Preparation method

For the mackerel:
Pick mackerel and place in a bowl with sour cream and finely chopped chives and chilli. Add salt to taste. Mix with a fork.

For the crostini:
Slice French bread, put in oven with olive oil and salt until crisp and toasty.

Allow to cool and then present them on a plate with a nice handful of green leaf salad (to dress with salt pepper and olive oil just before you serve.

Marinated peppers bruschetta
by Helly Kage

'Lovely recipe, for lovely times! It's simple but impressive. It's good, but healthy. My friends always love it when I make some, and the peppers also remind me of snails – probably why I love it so much!'

Ingredients

- 2 peppers (or more) for a cheerful result use different colours!
- 2 garlic cloves
- 3 tbsp extra virgin olive oil
- 2 sprigs of parsley
- salt & pepper

Preparation method

Roast the peppers in the oven until their skin turns brown (don't worry if it looks burnt), for approximately thirty to forty minutes depending on the heat.

Remove from the oven and cool. When you can touch the peppers without burning yourself, skin them, remove the seeds and cut them into thin slices (one to two cms).

Place the slices in a jar or tupperware container, in the olive oil you have already mixed with crushed garlic, finely chopped parsley, salt and pepper.

Stir the peppers into the mixture. Don't be afraid of using too much oil, it should cover all the slices for a better marinade.

Place in the fridge for at least two hours.

Serve cold with warm toasted bread.

Guacamole
by Gabriel de Villaines

'My cousin Alix came back from Mexico after spending a year in the capital city. She's the one who taught me how to make guacamole. Since then, I've been doing it very often every time people come to our house for a drink... and everybody loves it!'

Preparation method

Skin the avocado and mash it up with a fork. Cut the tomato into tiny squares without peeling it.

Cut the onion into tiny squares as well and add it to the mashed avocado. Mix without blending too much.

Squeeze the lemon onto the mixture and add the salt, pepper, two drops of tabasco sauce and a bit of paprika powder.

It's ready! And it's delicious with nachos...

Ingredients

- 1 ripe avocado
- 1 tomato
- 1 onion
- 1 lime
- salt, pepper, tabasco, paprika

Emergency Meals & T.V. Dinners

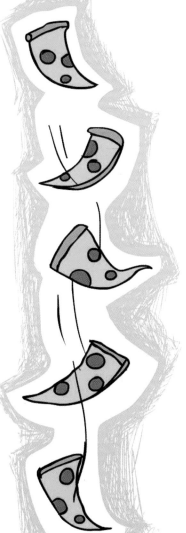

Emergency! Emergency! It's late and you've nothing to eat, and no idea what to cook either. All you want to do is crash on your sofa and watch a movie. A take-away meal is oh-so-tempting. No matter how much it costs and whether it tastes like sawdust, you simply can't be bothered to cook anything. Or can you?

Come on, it won't take long. We know you just want to chill out but think of the marvels that await you! The pleasure you'll get from grating cheese on your pizza, from fresh mince meat in your chilli, from real veg in your quiche!

There's no stopping you now as you run towards the kitchen, cookbook in hand, ready to knock up a mouth-watering TV dinner...

Don't stop! Don't look back! Run, RUN!

Pesto cherry tomato pie
(gluten and dairy free)
by Shaz Bloggs

'This is a very yummy recipe, but it's only dairy free if you make the pesto yourself without parmesan, which I usually do – still tastes great!'

Preparation method

Dough:

Mix all the dry ingredients in a large bowl. Add the egg and oil. Mix well.

Add water progressively: there is enough when you can form a ball that does not stick to your fingers. Wrap the ball in clingfilm, and put in the fridge for an hour.

Pre-heat your oven to 200°C. Spread the pastry out on grease proof paper (sprinkle with flour if sticky) and place it in a round dish. Stab holes into the pastry with a fork. Put a second sheet of grease proof paper over the top, and fill it with nuts (with their shells on, eg almonds). Put the dish in the oven and bake for thirty to forty minutes.

Topping:

Spread the pesto all over the pastry. Put the cherry tomatoes on top of the pesto.

Whisk the eggs in a bowl and add the cream, salt, pepper and nutmeg. Mix well. Pour the preparation over the tomatoes and sprinkle with grated cheese.

Bake in the oven at 200°C for thirty minutes, or until the base is golden.

Ingredients *serves 4*

Dough
- 100g rice flour
- 100g maize flour
- 1 tsp salt
- 1 pinch baking powder
- 2 eggs
- 5ml olive oil
- almonds
- water

Topping
- 4 tbsp pesto
- 500g cherry tomatoes halved (or 3 big tomatoes)
- 3 eggs
- 2 tbsp soya cream
- 1 tsp nutmeg
- dairy free cheese (optional)
- salt & pepper

Fish curry
by Salim Vijri

'This dish is a personal favourite for its simplicity but real depth of flavour, if the spices are balanced right. Being half Indian, I was brought up with this kind of fresh and aromatic cooking!'

Ingredients
serves 2-3

- fresh coley fillet (cod can be used), skinless
- 1 red onion
- 2 spring onions
- fresh coriander
- basmati rice
- 1 garlic clove
- spices: fennel seeds, coriander seeds, garam masala, turmeric,
- handful of pistachio nuts
- coconut milk
- pre-made curry paste
- red chilli
- lemon and lime
- salt & pepper

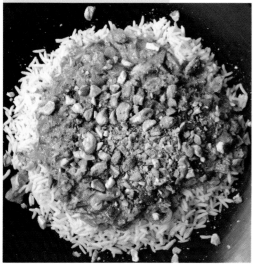

Preparation method

For the spiced rice:
Heat a dash of olive oil in a pan on a low heat. Add whole fennel seeds and turmeric and allow to slowly cook. When you smell the spices frying, add the rice to the pan and mix with the spices. Allow this to gently fry until the rice glistens.

Add boiling water to just cover the rice and add a lid to the pan. Allow the rice to cook on a medium heat for six to seven minutes. When the rice is done, stir with a fork to separate the grains.

For the curry :
Cover the fish in the curry paste on both sides, but keep some paste on the side for later.

Add olive oil to a medium frying pan and set to medium heat. Throw in ground fennel seeds, coriander seeds, garam masala and allow to gently fry.

Add the fish and cook for ten minutes, turning as it cooks. Then turn the heat up and add chopped spring onions with finely chopped red onions. Allow the onions to soften then add more paste, coconut milk, fresh coriander and some chilli.

Allow this to cook on a medium to high heat for a few minutes until the fish appears to be flaking apart. Taste sauce and add a squeeze of either lemon or lime depending on your taste. Add crushed pistachio nuts on top.

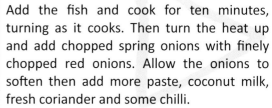

Papa's fresh sausage stew
by Janek Flemyng

'This recipe is very easy and very cheap. It doesn't take long to make and reminds you of childhood family meals. It's also banging before a night out.'

Preparation method

Sweat the onions, garlic and red pepper in a good amount of olive oil on a low heat until soft but not coloured.

Add the carrots and the sausages and cook for seven minutes.

Add the chopped tomatoes, the stock and the oregano and bring to the boil. Once bubbling, reduce the heat and simmer for thirty minutes.

Meanwhile, in a separate pan, cook the pasta in salted boiling water. When almost *al dente*, (ie firm but tender) drain and add to the sauce.

Add the cream, if using, and the butter to thicken the sauce then add the parsley and the lemon. Serve hot with parmesan and a drizzle of olive oil.

Ingredients
serves 4

• 2 large white onions, finely chopped
• 2 carrots, chopped
• 1 red pepper, finely chopped
• 6-8 Cumberland sausages, cut into 4-5 pieces per sausage (depending on size), skin left on
• 1 tin of chopped tomatoes
• 3 cloves of garlic
• handful of parsley, roughly chopped
• 200 ml pork stock
• a squeeze of lemon
• 1 tsp dried oregano
• 1 tbsp double cream or crème fraiche
• 1 packet of Rigatoni pasta
• 1 small knob of butter
• good olive oil
• salt & pepper

Raf's revolutionary pizza
by Rafal Zawistowski

'We learnt how to make this pizza at school and it's delicious. At first I thought making a pizza would be difficult but it's not. It's actually pretty easy, which is good, because it's my favourite food!'

Ingredients
serves 3-4

Pizza dough:
- 500g flour
- 50g flour for dusting
- 7g sachet of yeast
- 1/2 tsp salt
- 1 pinch of pepper
- 1 tsp dried basil
- 250 ml water
- 2 tbsp olive oil

Topping:
- 250g crushed tomato purée
- 1 tsp dried basil
- 1 yellow/orange/red pepper
- ¼ onion
- 1 tomato
- 250g chorizo sausage
- 150g buffalo mozzarella

Preparation method

Mix the pepper, salt, yeast, basil and flour in the mixing bowl. Slowly pour in half the water while mixing the flour. Then add the oil while continuing to stir and then slowly add the rest of the water to the mixture.

Place the lump of dough onto a wooden cutting board or surface. Knead using the extra dusting flour until the dough becomes a smooth ball. Let it rest for a while and turn the oven to 200°C on a fan setting if possible.

Finely chop the pepper, onion and chorizo and finely slice the tomato. Lightly glaze the baking sheet and then spread out the dough onto it. Spread out the tomato paste evenly across the surface of the pizza. Sprinkle with the dried basil and then start to add the topping. Place the onion and chorizo on first, then add the pepper. Tear the mozzarella into small chunks and spread across the pizza. Finally, put on the tomato slices.

Bake at 200°C for twenty-five minutes or until the dough has cooked through. Cut the pizza up and eat with your hands if you wish!

Clare's completely yummy chilli con carne
by Clare Gosling

'This recipe is perfect when served with a big bag of plain tortilla crisps and around two ounces of rice per person!'

Preparation method

Chop up the carrots and fry them in the butter in a big pan. Add in the chopped onion and garlic, then the courgette and pepper and finally the mushrooms. Now cook the mince on medium heat, adding in the stock cubes when the mince starts to brown. When it's cooked add the chopped tomatoes and then the whole can of red kidney beans with the water it comes in.

Now all of the ingredients are simmering away nicely, sprinkle on the salt, black pepper, hot chilli powder, dried basil, turmeric and paprika, as well as the fresh basil (finely chopped) keeping a little for later. Stir in well – if there is any excess liquid keep the heat on it to reduce; when it's a good thick consistency, add in a teaspoon of cornflour and then pop the pan into the oven at about 180°C for about twenty minutes.

Fry the rice for one to two minutes in a little oil until it starts to go slightly translucent, then add the water (two measures of water per one of rice). Put on a low temperature for fifteen minutes with the lid on (check to see if all the water has been absorbed – if not turn the heat up for a minute or two) then take it off the heat, remove the lid and put a teatowel over the top. Leave for five minutes.

Spoon the chilli con carne mixture into bowls. Sprinkle a few of the leftover fresh basil leaves on top and put a handful of tortilla chips on the side. Serve with rice.

Ingredients   *serves 4*

Chilli:
- 2 carrots
- 3 garlic cloves, chopped
- 1 courgette
- 1 white onion
- 1 red onion
- 2 cans plum tomatoes
- 1 can red kidney beans
- 500g lean mince meat
- 1 yellow, orange or red pepper
- 200g chestnut mushrooms
- butter

Seasoning:
- 3 pinches salt
- large sprinkling ground black pepper or several grinds fresh ground pepper
- large sprinkling hot chilli powder
- large sprinkling dried basil
- heaped tsp turmeric
- large sprinkling paprika
- bunch fresh basil leaves finely chopped
- 2 beef stock cubes (sprinkled)

Vegan Pie
by Rob Matty

'This recipe is quite cool because it uses silken tofu, and to be honest, it's the only thing I can cook where I get to use this ingredient.'

Preparation method

Pastry: Mix the flour, salt and veggie butter with your hands until the mixture is crumbly. Add the water very slowly, mixing with a fork until homogeneous. Form a ball and start kneading it. Press pastry flat and lay on a pie plate. Wrap in clingfilm and keep in the fridge until the filling is ready.

Filling: Heat the oil in a pan and add the chopped onion, garlic and leek. Put a lid on and cook it on a medium heat for five minutes. Finely chop the kale and roughly chop the mushrooms then add them, stirring everything round. Pop the lid on and leave to cook or around five minutes. Now add the Worcestershire sauce, mustard, parsley and the salt and pepper. Stir it round and give it half a minute to cook together.

Ingredients *serves 4*

Pastry:
• 3/4 cup unbleached white flour
• 3/4 cup whole wheat / spelt flour
• 1/2 tbsp salt
• 2/3 cup veggie spread
• 1/2 cup ice water

Filling:
• 2 tbsp cooking oil
• 1 leek - or 2 (white parts only)
• 1 small onion
• 250g mushrooms
• 1 large handful kale
• 3 cloves garlic
• 2 tsp Worcestershire sauce
• 1 tsp dried parsley
• salt & pepper

Soy 'icing':
• 300g silken tofu
• 125ml soya milk
• sunflower seeds

Soy 'icing': Blend the tofu and the soya milk into a paste. Add a pinch of salt and some mixed herbs (and some powdered chilli if you like). Spread the paste evenly on top of the filling. Place the sunflower seeds in a pan and heat gently until the seeds start to brown. When they're ready, sprinkle them on top of the pie. Place the pie in the oven at 180°C and check on it regularly for twenty-five to thirty-five minutes until fully cooked.

Chicken soup express and cheese muffins with bits in
by Roscoe Savage

'This is great if you need quick comfort food while busy with essays or exams. If you are in a real hurry you can miss out some of the seasoning and use a packet of chicken noodles! The bits in the cheese muffins can be any leftover ingredients. A great recipe for using up what you find in the fridge.'

Ingredients

serves 4

Soup:
• 1 litre chicken stock
• 3 chicken breasts cut into thin strips
• 3 spring onions sliced fine
• 100g frozen peas
• few green beans sliced
• little gem lettuce sliced
• 200g fast cook noodles (or 2 packs 2 min noodles)
• 2 tsp soy
• 2 tsp hoi sin sauce
• salt & pepper

Muffins:
• 85g polenta
• 125ml milk (works well with sour milk)
• 225g self-raising flour
• 1 tbsp sugar
• 125g can creamed sweetcorn
• 2 eggs
• 30g grated cheese
• 3 rashers cooked bacon
• 4 spring onions, chopped
• 50g cheese

Preparation method

For the soup:
The hardest part of this is cutting everything up nice and small. Bring the stock to the boil and keep it boiling for six minutes. Add the chicken and simmer for five minutes. Add everything else and simmer until noodles are cooked. Serve in bowls with spoons and chopsticks.

For the muffins:
Make everything apart from the bacon, onions and sweetcorn into a thick batter and stir in.

Add the bacon, onions and sweetcorn and spoon into muffin tins (greased or lined). Cut 50g cheese into twelve cubes and push one into each muffin before baking at 180°C for twenty minutes. Serve warm.

Fish pie
by Yobidiah Livinstoney

'My grandma used to make this when I was a kid and it was one of my favourite things to eat. It's the only recipe she ever taught me. It's big and warm and comforting for winter when it's cold outside.'

Ingredients

- 1kg potatoes
- 1 ½ pints of milk
- 200g cheese (grated)
- 250g peeled prawns
- 500g fish
- 600g carrots
- 600g swede
- 600g cabbage
- fresh parsley (chopped)
- 3 heaped tbsp butter
- a little flour
- 1 tbsp mustard
- 2 tbsp Worcestershire sauce
- salt & pepper

Preparation method

Chop the potatoes and boil them. Cut up the veg into one cm cubes and fry them up together in a bit of oil. Preheat the oven to 200°C. Take the fish and cut it up (it's best to use a mixture if you can – I usually use trout fillets and smoked mackerel). Put it in a large pot along with the prawns. When the veg is cooked, add to the pot and mix together.

Take two heaped tablespoons of butter and melt it in a pan. Add an equal amount of flour and mix it in. Next add a little milk and stir it so there are no lumps. Keep adding the milk, stirring slowly, keeping just a little back for the mash.

Add salt and pepper, parsley, mustard, the Worcestershire sauce and the cheese. Keep stirring on a gentle heat until nice and thick. Make the mash with the leftover butter and milk. A thick mash is better than a thin mash for this.

Add the cheese sauce to the veg and fish and mix together. Then spread the mash on top evenly. Drag a fork over the top of the potato so you get nice lines across the top. Put the pie in the oven for twenty minutes. It's ready when the potato is going golden. Switch the oven to grill for the last few minutes to really get it brown and crispy. Now serve straight away but watch your mouth. The American Army first came up with the idea of Napalm after one of their Generals burnt himself while eating a fish pie during the Second World War. You have been warned!!

Seafood lasagna
by Kojo Koram

'I like this recipe because I am a secret merman and this reminds of my home life under the sea!'

Ingredients
serves 4

- 250g prawns,
- 250g mixed seafood (scallops, crayfish, mussels etc)
- 2 salmon steaks
- pre-cooked lasagna sheets
- 1 pint of milk
- a variety of cheeses
- flour
- 1 pot of single cream
- 1 tsp mustard
- 1 bag of spinach
- onions, garlic and green peppers to taste
- salt & pepper

Preparation method

Fry all the seafood with onions, garlic and peppers for ten minutes. Continually turn the seafood over to ensure it is well cooked. Add salt and pepper to taste.

In a separate saucepan, start to melt a teaspoon of butter. When that is almost melted, add the flour and fry. Add some olive oil over the top and continually mix until it all turns golden brown. This should take about five to eight minutes. Once brown, slowly add the milk and mix it all together.

Once the flour and milk are combined, add the mustard, cream and cheese.

Continually mix until you make a nice creamy sauce.

Take out a baking tray. Make a layer of the lasagna sheets at the bottom of the tray.

Then add a layer of the seafood on top.
Pour the cream sauce over it. Repeat this process until the layers are complete. Finish with a layer of the lasagna sheets with some cheese sprinkled on top.

Leave in the oven at 215°C for thirty minutes or until cooked to satisfaction.

Sweet Treats That Are Good For You

Desserts! Cookies, brownies, ice cream, chocolate sauce melting on juicy strawberries... experience an explosion of flavours and colours, of aromas and shapes!

As you lick your fingers and open your cupboard, the honey and sugar smile at you. They're ready... Are you?

The days when you could bite into a dry, factory-made biscuit with pleasure are long gone. Now you need more. You deserve more... all the time you were buying those tasteless processed cakes, these treats were waiting in the wings. But now the time has come to get baking!

So go ahead, get cracking those eggs! Let your taste buds take a journey to the land of homemade nectar!

Banana mousse
by Corantin Travers

'Ok, so this recipe is quite simple once you get used to making it, but I have to say it can be rather tricky the first time. I think the most important thing is: take your time when you add the egg whites. Do it really slowly, and it should be ok. And even if it's not, this mousse is really worth trying again!'

Preparation method

Separate the egg whites and the yokes. Mix the sugar and the yolks and stir until the mixture turns white. Add one cup of cold milk. Stir until the sugar dissolves.

Add three tablespoons of flour and three cups of hot milk. Mix together. Put the mixture in a pan and bring to the boil for three minutes.

Remove from the heat. Add a teaspoon of vanilla flavouring. Add four or five sliced bananas.

Whisk egg whites until very stiff (otherwise some of the mousse turns watery) and add to the mixture, slowly stirring by lifting the egg whites with a spoon. Be very careful not to break the egg whites.

And it's ready! If you want you can also add some melted chocolate on top of the mousse, or some cocoa powder.

This mousse does not keep so consume within a few hours!

Ingredients

- 6 eggs
- 3 tbsp flour
- 12 tbsp sugar
- 1 tbsp vanilla flavour
- 4 cups milk
- 4 or 5 bananas
- dark chocolate (optional)

Pain de gene (Almond cake)
by Laurane Marchive

'This is a cake my mother used to make a lot. And I think it's my favourite ever. It seems almost impossible to mess it up and it's just delicious. Maybe not the healthiest cake ever but hey, we all need to indulge a bit from time to time...'

Preparation method

Line a cake tin with greaseproof paper and smear with butter.

Using a blender, blend the almonds together with half the sugar.

Meanwhile, mix the butter and the rest of the sugar. Using a fork, soften the mixture until it turns creamy.

Mix this together with the blended almonds. Add the eggs one by one, stirring vigorously.

Then add the salt, the flour and your choice of flavouring.

Pour the mixture into the tin!

Cook for about forty to fifty minutes at a very moderate heat of 150°C.

Ingredients

- 150g sugar
- 125g butter
- 40g flour
- 100g almonds (you need ones with their brown skins on)
- 3 eggs
- 1/4 tsp salt
- 1 shot of kirsch, rum or any other flavouring

Oat biscuits
by Jack Lowe

'Excellent cookies and super simple to make!'

Preparation method

Preheat the oven at 180°C and grease your baking tray.

Weigh the flour and oats and place in a mixing bowl. Add sugar and raisins. Add butter. Rub together until the whole mixture is combined.

Add cinnamon, nutmeg and syrup and mix together.

Form the mixture into balls and place on the baking tray. Slightly flatten the mixture.

Place on the top shelf of the oven and bake for fifteen to twenty minutes.

Remove from the oven and let them cool on the cooling rack for twenty minutes.

Ingredients

- 75g rolled oats
- 125g self-raising flour
- 100g margarine
- 50g soft brown sugar
- 2 x 20ml tsp syrup
- 50g raisins
- cinnamon and nutmeg

Chocolate and raspberries fondant
by Felipe Terazzan

'This cake tastes best after a few hours or the next day, so it is recommended that you bake in the morning or the day before. If you like my recipe and want to find more, check out my website! www.theblindtaste.com'

Preparation method

Set the oven to 190°C. Line an eight inch round cake tin with greaseproof paper. Cut the butter into cubes and break the dark chocolate into small pieces. Melt them together in a *bain marie* (or you can use a small saucepan on top of a larger one full of boiling water). Stir regularly until perfectly mixed.

Once the butter and chocolate are melted remove from the heat and allow to cool for a few minutes. Scrape the butter and chocolate into a larger bowl and stir in the sugar. Add the eggs one by one, always stirring.

Once the mixture is ready, scrape it into the lined tin. After washing the raspberries, break the white chocolate into tiny squares and place them alternately into the mixture, one raspberry then one chocolate square, making a line.

Bake for twenty-one minutes.

Ingredients

- 200g dark chocolate
- 100g white chocolate
- 200g granulated sugar
- 200g unsalted butter
- 4 eggs
- raspberries

Pear and almond tart
by Dominic McInnes

'I love cooking this tart because I have noticed baking is the best way to bring people together. And there's nothing better than sharing a good cake with friends – it makes me happy every time!'

Preparation method

Slice the pears lengthways. Separate the egg whites from the yolks, and whisk until frothy.

Sift the icing sugar and flour into a bowl, and stir in the ground almonds.

Mix in the egg whites and melted butter, and stir together.

Pour mixture into a (greased) baking tin.

Place pears on top, and then the flaked almonds.

Bake for twenty or thirty minutes, or until base is firm and springy.

Eat!

Ingredients

- 7oz icing sugar
- 3oz plain flour
- 5oz ground almonds
- 5 egg whites
- 7oz butter, melted
- 3 pears
- flaked almonds

Minute choco cookies
by Amelia Wells

'These cookies combat oppression and if you don't make them vegan then you're destroying the planet, so weep for your future!!'

Ingredients

• 2oz butter (for vegan variation use Vitalite or other dairy free spread)
• 4oz brown sugar (muscovado is good)
• 6oz dark chocolate
• 8oz plain flour
• pinch baking powder

Preparation method

Beat the sugar and butter together.

Melt the chocolate (but leave a little bit not quite melted for chocolate chips).

Add the chocolate to the sugar and butter.

Sift flour in and stir.

Roll into little balls and bake for ten to twelve minutes at around 160°C.

They're ready!

Tapioca pudding
by Sarah Eisenfisz

'I love this dessert because it reminds me of my childhood. When I was little, my mum often made it for me and now it's really cool to make it for other people. It doesn't require too many ingredients, which is always a good thing when you feel too lazy to go to the shop...'

Ingredients

- 3 cups milk (animal or vegetable e.g. soya, rice, almond milk...)
- 1/3 cup pearl tapioca
- 1/3 cup cane sugar
- 1/4 tsp sea salt
- flavour (vanilla, orange blossom, almond, cacao, coconut...)

Preparation method

In a medium-sized saucepan, pour in all the ingredients and slowly bring to the boil on a medium heat, while stirring with a wooden spoon.

The mixture will progressively get thicker and the pearls will become gradually transparent.

When the milk has been completely absorbed by the tapioca, pour the cream into individual ramekins (or small dessert dishes).

This tapioca pudding tastes very good when served warm but it's delicious cold as well, as the pudding turns into a stiffer cream consistency as it cools.

Carrot cake
by Pia Himmelstern

'I like this carrot cake recipe because everyone thinks it's awful, but in the end, everyone loves it! My advice: eat it with smarties, it's even more enjoyable!'

Preparation method

Heat up the oven to 190°C.

Place the carrots in boiling water and cook them for about fifteen minutes. When cooked, cool them down under cold water. Slice the carrots.

Add four eggs and one cup of oil (tea cup). Mix it altogether.

Add two cups of sugar (tea cup), one cup of flour (tea cup) and one teaspoonful of baking powder to the mixture.

Mix everything together smoothly and put it into a baking tray in the oven for thirty minutes, at 190°C. When cooked, remove and let it cool. Enjoy!

Ingredients

- 3 carrots
- 4 eggs
- 1 cup oil
- 2 cups sugar
- 1 cup flour
- 1 tsp baking powder

Snacks & Smoothies

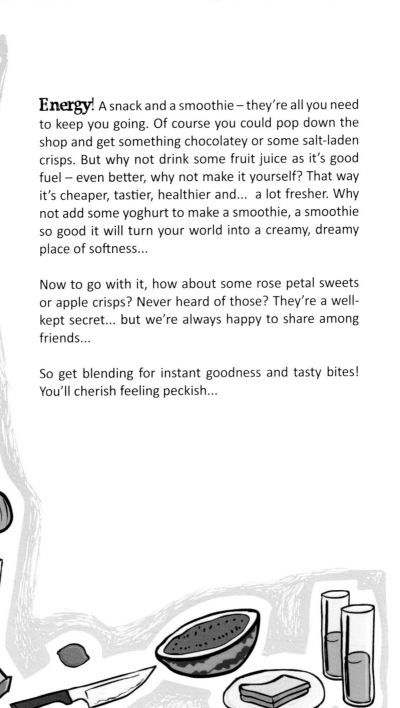

Energy! A snack and a smoothie – they're all you need to keep you going. Of course you could pop down the shop and get something chocolatey or some salt-laden crisps. But why not drink some fruit juice as it's good fuel – even better, why not make it yourself? That way it's cheaper, tastier, healthier and... a lot fresher. Why not add some yoghurt to make a smoothie, a smoothie so good it will turn your world into a creamy, dreamy place of softness...

Now to go with it, how about some rose petal sweets or apple crisps? Never heard of those? They're a well-kept secret... but we're always happy to share among friends...

So get blending for instant goodness and tasty bites! You'll cherish feeling peckish...

Rose petal sweets
by Camille Leloire

'These sweets are really easy to make and they can be a perfect snack! I love them because they're so unusual... I guess we're not used to eating flowers that much! It's actually a really good "recipe" if you have a garden or homegrown roses, as you wouldn't want to eat the pesticides on industrial flowers...'

Ingredients

- 3 organic or home-grown roses
- 1 egg white
- caster sugar (preferably white as it looks better at the end, but you can use brown sugar too if that's all you've got)

Preparation method

Carefully pluck up the rose petals and wash them with cold water. Make sure there are no insects left on the petals.

Put your egg white in a bowl and add enough sugar for the mixture to get slightly sticky. I usually add between three and five tablespoons.

One by one, dip the petals in the egg white and lay them on greaseproof paper. The petals have to be covered with just a thin layer of egg white, no more.

When all your petals are on the grease-proof paper, use a sieve to sprinkle sugar on the petals.

Leave the petals to dry for one or two hours and delicately turn them on the other side. Sprinkle sugar again.

When the petals are harder on both sides, it means they are ready! You can keep them in a bowl somewhere and make sure they stay dry.

You can have them as snacks, but you can also use them to decorate cakes. They look brilliant! *Bon appetit!*

Apple crisps
by Laurent Quintal

'This is a really good snack and easy to make, especially when you have got apples sitting somewhere in a cupboard getting old. Just stick them in the oven and you can make delicious crisps.'

Ingredients

- 5 apples
- cinnamon (or any other spice you like)
- sugar

Preparation method

Pre-heat your oven to 170°C.

Slice the apples, making the slices as thin as possible and discarding the ends.

Place the slices on baking paper and sprinkle sugar and cinnamon on them.

Put the tray in the oven, on a very low heat, and bake for two to three hours. Turn them midway to make sure they get crispy all the way through.

You can then store the crisps for several days in a dry place.

Summer veggie toast
by Jeremy Lickery

'This is the easiest way to trick people into thinking you can make starters, and it's also a tasty goat-y snack.'

Ingredients

- 1 clove of garlic
- 1 courgette
- plain muffins
- passata
- tomato purée
- soft goat's cheese
- olive oil
- fresh basil

Preparation method

Cut each muffin in half and lightly toast (two halves per person is good for a snack/ starter).

Cut the courgette in half and then cut each half long-ways into slivers. Drizzle with olive oil and place under a medium grill until slightly browned.

Meanwhile fry the finely chopped garlic in olive oil for several minutes then add the passata. Leave to simmer until slightly reduced, adding the tomato purée to thicken. You should heat enough passata to cover each muffin. When ready, spread the passata on the muffins before adding a knob of goat's cheese and the slivers of courgette.

Finally, place under the grill until the goat's cheese has just started to melt. Sprinkle with the basil leaves before serving.

After party smoothie
by Tommy Labuttiere

'My favourite smoothie after a night out. When you're tired and dehydrated, there's nothing better than ginger and watermelon. This smoothie takes less than five minutes to make so you can make loads of it really easily, and it'll help you recover from anything.'

Preparation method

Remove the skin and the seeds of the watermelon and cut it into big chunks. Blend it.

Slice up an apple (you don't need to peel it) and add it in the blender. Cut off the skin of the ginger and add it as well. Blend everything.

If your blender is also an ice-crusher, you can add crushed ice to the smoothie.

Well I guess that's it. Just drink, enjoy and recover!

Ingredients

- 1/4 watermelon
- 1 apple
- 1 little piece of ginger

Banana smoothie
by Alex Mckechnie

'My milkshake brings all the boys (and girls) to the backyard – and they're absolutely right about it being better than yours! Hehehehehehehehehehe!'

Preparation method

Well... not much of a method here. Just take everything and put it in the blender.

Blend and drink! What else...?

Honey

Ingredients

- 2 scoops frozen yoghurt
- 300ml milk
- 1 banana
- 50 ml honey
- 1/2 tsp ground nutmeg

Veggie juice
by Barry Hallinger

'Vegetables, vegetables, vegetables, I love vegetables. In juices, in cakes, everywhere. They are full of vitamins and they taste great. In a smoothie they're even better as you're eating them raw. A good way to get your five a day!'

Preparation method

Peel the carrot, the cucumber and the orange.

You don't need to peel the apple, just make sure you get rid of the core.

Chop up the carrot, cucumber, apple, orange and tomato in big chunks. Put them all in a blender.

Add a little bit of honey and blend everything for a few minutes until perfectly liquified.

Squeeze the lemon on top, and serve cold!

Ingredients

- 1 carrot
- 1 cucumber
- 1 tomato
- 1 orange
- 1 apple
- 1/2 lemon
- honey to taste

D.I.Y.

Do do do, do do do do! DO IT YOURSELF!!!

If you're tired of paying too much money for a jar of processed peanut butter or a tub of bland, unexciting hummus, follow us on the path to homemade delicacies.

You never knew you could make ketchup, did you? Have you ever dreamt of making your own chocolate spread? It's fun and delicious too!

Surprise your friends when you offer them a mind-blowing energy bar, toast with remarkable rhubarb jam, a hot snack with your own brand of spicy chutney or a tuna sandwich with fresh mayonnaise...

Hummus
by Eric Pradeux

'Yummy! Yummy! This is so easy to do! My mum showed me how to make it once, and now I want it all the time! It's a good snack and it's better when you do it yourself, rather than when you buy it from a shop!'

Ingredients

- 400g canned chickpeas (drained)
- 2 tsp olive oil
- 2 tsp lemon juice
- 2 garlic cloves
- paprika
- cumin,
- (optional: 3 tsp tahina and sesame butter)
- salt & pepper

Preparation method

Mix the chickpeas with the lemon juice, olive oil, tahina and crushed garlic cloves, until it becomes a smooth paste. Add salt, pepper, pinches of paprika and cumin (to taste)

Keep it in the fridge and serve cool on warm pitta bread or toast.

Mmmm!

Rhubarb jam
by Francis Magnal

'A good old school jam for the lazies. You almost don't have anything to do, except for watching the whole thing cook and get all sweet. And it's much better than the one you buy! I highly recommend it.'

Ingredients

- 400g rhubarb
- 200g to 300g sugar (depending on how sweet you like your jam!)
- vanilla flavour

Preparation method

Peel the rhubarb (don't bother using a knife, just do it with your nails).

Cut the rhubarb into three cm pieces and place them in a pan. Cover them with the sugar, add the vanilla and leave them for at least one hour.

Once in a while, stir the rhubarb. It should become soft and start producing water.

After one or two hours, put the pan on a low heat. The longer you left the rhubarb in the sugar, the shorter the time it will take to cook.

Just make sure you stir the mixture regularly and keep an eye on it. It should be cooked when the rhubarb turns yellowish.

To know wether your jam is cooked you can also drop a little bit on a plate. If it solidifies straight away, it means it's ready! Let it cool down and pour into a sealed jar.

Zingy tomato sauce
by Gabriel Magnal

Ketchup is usually regarded as junk food because it contains loads of sugar and preservatives and weird other stuff. But I love it! So I've learnt to make my own, much healthier than the ones you can buy!

Preparation method

Pour boiling hot water on the tomatoes and leave for a few minutes. Then peel them (the heat should make it easier to take off their skin). When peeled, blend the tomatoes.

Meanwhile, peel and chop the onions, put them in a frying pan with a little bit of oil and cook them on a low heat for about ten minutes.

In a big pan, mix the blended tomatoes, onions, sugar, salt and vinegar and cook on a low heat for about an hour. The mixture should never burn but it should progressively thicken.

When it's thick, blend it again then put it in another pan and cover it with a cloth.

Let it cool down for about two hours. The longer you leave it with the cloth on, the stronger the flavour will be.

Then put it in a bottle, and it's ready! It will keep for up to three weeks.

Ingredients

- 12 medium size tomatoes
- 1 onion
- 80g sugar
- 80g white wine vinegar
- 2 tbsp olive oil
- 1/2 tsp salt

Mind-blowing chocolate spread
by Sophie Desfleur

'This is a good alternative to the well-known chocolate spreads you can find in supermarkets; it's much much healthier as at least you know exactly what's in it!'

Ingredients

- 200g toasted hazelnuts
- 400ml whole milk
- 50g powdered skimmed milk
- 3 tbsp honey
- 200g milk chocolate, broken up
- 100g dark chocolate, broken up
- pinch of salt

Preparation method

In a pan, heat up the milk, powdered milk, honey and salt. When it starts boiling, take away from the heat.

Microwave the chocolate to melt it, or place it in a pan plunged into a bigger pan full of water. The chocolate has to melt and form a paste.

Place the hazelnuts in a blender and blend them until they turn into powder. You can blend thoroughly if you don't want chunks, but if you do, make sure you stop blending before they're all thoroughly ground.

Pour the warm chocolate into the blender. Blend. From time to time, shake the blender to make sure everything gets mixed together. The chocolate paste can sometimes get stuck on the sides and too far away from the blades. If that happens, take a knife and scrape the sides to push it back to the bottom.

When the preparation is thoroughly mixed, add the warm milk. Blend again until smooth.

You can then pour the mixture into one or more jars, depending on their size. It might be quite runny when it's finished, but that doesn't matter as the chocolate will solidify after a few hours in the fridge.

And you can keep it for up to nine days. Although it will probably be eaten before!

Peanut butter
by Tom Grundy

'Super easy to make and super-tasty. You can make it with salt or with sugar, you can have it on toast, in sandwiches, anywhere... I love peanut butter and it's good fun to prepare it instead of buying it!

Ingredients

- 300g monkey nuts
- 6 tbsp oil
- salt or sugar

Preparation method

Open the monkey nuts and place the shelled peanuts on a lightly greased baking tray.

Set the oven to 180°C .
Cook the nuts for fifteen to twenty minutes. Stir them once or twice during cooking time.

When the peanuts are cooked, let them cool down for about ten minutes.

Then rub them between your fingers in order to take off their thin, brown skins. The skin should come off easily.

Put the peanuts in a blender and add six tablespoons of oil. Blend it all together.

You can add some sugar or salt to taste, if you want sweet or savoury peanut butter. Or you can just have it as it is.

Enjoy!

Energy bars
by Elly Pradinat

'Energy bars are perfect when you go trekking, or when you've got exams, or when you just need rich, easy food, but the bars they sell in supermarkets are often packed with preservatives, that's why I like to make my own. You can adapt them to your taste, change the fruits, the nuts or the cereal!'

Preparation method

Pre-heat your oven to 170°C.

In a pan, mix the butter, the honey and the sugar. Stir continuously and add the cereal, the almonds and the dried fruits.

When the mixture is thick, spread it in a square cake tin, preferably a non-stick one as it will be easier to take the mixture out. Make sure the mixture is evenly spread and well pressed down all over. Put it in the oven and cook for about twenty-five minutes.

When cooked, put the mixture in the fridge and allow to cool for a few hours, until perfectly solid. You can then take it out of the tin and cut it into bars.

When cut, wrap the bars in tinfoil and keep them in the fridge.

They'll keep for up to a week!

Ingredients

- 50g sugar
- 50g honey
- 100 g butter
- 125g dried fruit
- 100g crushed almonds
- 100g cereal

Chutney
by Will B. Sudney

'This chutney is the best ever. I always make huge quantities of it and keep it in jars for months. I never run out, that's for sure, and if you purchase your ingredients in the right place, it's also cheaper than buying good quality ready-made ones.'

Ingredients

- 5 large onions
- 2kg fresh tomatoes
- 3 large red peppers
- 500g sundried tomatoes (not in oil)
- 1 large bulb of garlic
- 3 bags of mixed chillies (approx. 50-70)
- 1 bottle of Haberno Tabasco sauce
- 1 pint of cider vinegar
- salt & pepper

Preparation method

Halve the tomatoes, and soak in a bowl of hot water for around fifteen minutes. Drain and chop roughly.

Roughly chop all of the other ingredients.

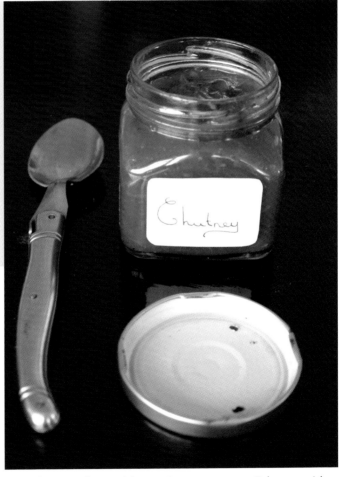

Gently fry onions, garlic and chilli, for approximately one to two minutes, then add tomatoes, peppers, Tabasco, cider vinegar and generous seasoning.

Stir continuously while bringing to simmering point, and leave on a low heat for around three hours (stirring occasionally to prevent sticking). Allow to cool then pour into jar.

Mayonnaise
by Arune Cepelyte

'Mayonnaise is so versatile. Add a little Truffle oil and finely chopped chives and you have a beautiful truffle mayonnaise for white fish or roast potatoes. Finely chop some gherkins, capers, garlic, parsley and hardboiled egg and you have a magnificent tartar sauce. Note the mayonnaise will not keep for more than one day because of the presence of raw egg; it is also not suitable for pregnant women or people with intolerance to lecithin.'

Preparation method

In a large bowl whisk together all ingredients except the oils. Gradually add the oil, spoon by spoon at first, whisking all the time so the mayonnaise emulsifies. Continue until the mayo is thick and gooey. If it is too thick add a splash of water. If it is too thin, whisk in a little more oil.

The mayo will split if:
1. The oil is too cold
2. The oil is added too quickly
3. There is not enough mustard in the mix

Ingredients

- 150ml sunflower oil
- 80ml olive oil
- splash of white wine vinegar
- 2 egg yolks
- 1 large tsp Dijon mustard
- seasoning

The mustard helps the emulsification. If the mayo splits, add a spoonful of mustard and a fresh egg yolk to a clean dry bowl.

Gradually trickle in the mayonnaise mix as before, nice and slowly.

Store in the fridge and use within the day.